THE PRO RETAIL TRADER

THE PRO RETAIL TRADER

How to Generate Professional-level Returns as a Retail Trader

Steve Ruffley

HARRIMAN HOUSE LTD
3 Viceroy Court
Bedford Road
Petersfield
Hampshire
GU32 3LJ
GREAT BRITAIN

Tel: +44 (0)1730 233870
Email: enquiries@harriman-house.com
Website: harriman.house

First published in 2024.

Paperback ISBN: 978-1-80409-137-1
eBook ISBN: 978-1-80409-138-8

British Library Cataloguing in Publication Data
A CIP catalogue record for this book can be obtained from the British Library.

Printed in India by Manipal Technologies Limited

For sale in the Indian subcontinent only

Dedicated to the pack:
The Ferret, Long Pig, Rat one & Otter Trotter.

CONTENTS

PREFACE

PRESUMABLY IF YOU are reading these words you are currently a trader, an aspiring trader or maybe just trade curious? No matter what kind of trader you think you are, or want to be, there are many statistics on the percentage of traders, especially retail traders, who fail. It's an unsurprisingly high number.

Why do people get involved in trading? To make money. Making money from trading is more than just a strategy. Look at it this way. If you return 100% in a year, you have beaten most hedge funds. If you have $25k starting capital, which I recommend starting with, then congratulations, you have doubled your money. However, you have probably earnt less than a fast-food employee, and maybe worked more hours doing so.

This book is about how I see trading differently. From what I have experienced and what I have done. From the retail world to that of the pro and everything in between. There is much more to making meaningful money trading than most people will ever realise.

This book is about intraday trading. I trade Forex (FX), the main indices and gold. While the practicalities of my trading – scalping and averaging – can be applied to any market that moves, like Bitcoin and individual stocks, I personally don't trade them. I don't take long-term trades. I don't make investments in the markets.

In this book I'm going to bridge the gap between the professional world of trading in which I was trained and that of retail where I now place these kinds of trades. I'm trying to dispel the myth of what people even think a pro trader is.

I have experience in both pro and retail trading. I have traded professionally on two of the biggest London floors. I've risk managed professional traders on the floor. I've managed a trading floor. I've been regulated by the FCA. I've educated thousands of retail traders and mentored many hundreds more.

To be clear, when I refer to the 'floor' I am talking about the electronic trading floors, not the 'live floors'.

Over the years I've traded my own money. I've traded clients' money. I've traded between 1 and 2,500 lots in seconds, minutes and hours. I have made big money from relatively big accounts, but also big money from small accounts, both professionally via the exchanges and on retail platforms.

I've taken all these insights and combined it with, in my opinion, my own personal defining trading quality: the ability to take pain.

I take extreme short-term pain in the markets. I actively force myself at times. Time is very important in my trading style and pain is most felt with my fade entry scalps.

You may not know what a fade entry scalp is yet. I guarantee if you have traded before then it is more than likely you will have traded one. You may have lost, or made very little money from it. Why? It's the easiest to spot and the most obvious in design to catch out traders.

I'm not trying to tell you that I'm some Zen trader who's always at one with the markets and my emotions, and have got the world of trading totally figured out. I don't. I've come to terms with how I need to interact with the markets in order to make money. I lose trades, I've lost lots of trades. It's simply part of trading. I've experienced the highs and lows just like every other trader, just probably with a few more noughts though.

I know myself. I'm only interested these days in making money from trading. Not being proven right. By making money I'm talking about amounts like $10,000 in two minutes, $77,000 in a couple of hours and $90,000 in a day.

I understand these amounts may seem inconceivable to some people.

I don't make these amounts all the time, but when I trade, I look to make thousands not hundreds. This is what professional traders do. When the right opportunities present themselves in the markets, they capitalise on them. Until you get to a certain level of size, a trade is just a trade. While scaling up seems one of the hardest things for traders to do, trading size is the only way I know to make each pip count.

Most people will never get to be a pro trader. Most retail traders, so the statistics tell you, fail.

I believe there is a space between the pro world and that of retail – a pro retail trader if you will.

This is what I am, this is how I trade.

MY TRADING JOURNEY

I GOT INVOLVED IN professional trading when I was living in Gibraltar, of all places. I fell into it the old-fashioned way, by happening to meet the right people.

I was taught to be a professional trader as part of an international Refco grad scheme. I was sent to London with my fellow grads to join a *Top Gun*-style trading academy in Refco's Liverpool Street offices. I say offices, but that doesn't really do it justice. It was a 150-desk trading floor with its own deli, gaming arcade and an underground parking lot full of super cars that would shame a sheik.

Now the *Top Gun* reference is there for effect, but they never put it in those terms. It does relate to me quite nicely a little later though, so just run with it.

Training traders is nothing new. Richard Dennis and William Eckhardt did this back in the '80s when they created their Turtle Traders. Refco had a more ruthless, corporate, Big Brother-esque approach. It was more like a TV show, like an early version of *The Apprentice*. We were all there to compete or be fired. That part is not for effect. We were told that if we didn't pass the periodic tests we would be fired, and people were.

During the day we were hammered with tests and detailed essays to write. A slew of theoretical trading and analysis scenarios to explain and present to the group. There was a reading list that consisted of every technical analysis book on the market. I must have spent a grand on books alone. It was a stream of constant testing and performing tasks.

This taught me a lot about the markets, a fair bit about trading, but little about making money or risk management. I didn't fully appreciate why they did it this way when I first started trading.

In hindsight it makes perfect sense to me now. They provided the education, the environment and capital. The hard part, making money and all that came with that, was down to you.

At night I would make a point of finding out where the top traders hung out and do what I do best, talk shop. This was a whole other type of education.

In the Square Mile when I was there, a trader was someone to be revered and respected. A young Andy Priston, or Braveheart as he was known, traded at Refco then. I was in the company of someone already making millions. I had my trading name picked out: Maverick. The *Top Gun* reference. I am a child of the '80s after all.

I passed the course and became a backed professional trader.

I had a great start to trading; on one occasion in my first few months I made £10k in a few hours.

To give you an idea what all this training and experience was worth to Refco, my initial buyout of being a backed trader was £250,000. That's how much you needed to pay back before you were free from your Refco contract.

(Of all the courses that ran, I personally knew of only one trader who did this – our paths would eventually cross again on the floor.)

I traded for a little over a year. After paying desk fees and withdrawals to live, I did not have a lot to show for what I thought was a considerable amount of time and effort.

I was a professional trader, but I wasn't making the living I wanted from being a trader.

I could make money. I could make winning trades. I could trade size when it counted, but I was missing something. I did not know how to get to the next level.

Luckily – and there is an element of luck in trading, or in my case, making your own luck – I was offered a position in the risk management room.

This was a pivotal moment in my trading journey.

Professional traders do not have the same attitude to risk as retail traders. Professional traders also do not have the same attitude to risk as the risk department. I can say with confidence, to anyone who has traded outside of a professional environment, you don't know how real-world, pro trading risk works with regards to making money.

I was able to see how some of the top traders made their money. I watched dozens of accounts trade simultaneously for well over a year. I got to see things very few traders, even pro traders, ever get to see.

What I saw changed everything for me. I didn't know if I could do it yet, but I knew what you had to do to make real money trading. Use more size.

Once you decide to be a trader, it can become an obsession. It certainly was for me. After I had got what I needed from my risk department experience, my only aim was to trade as I had seen.

Via an introduction, I set up a meeting to start trading at Schneider Trading Associates. This is where I met Sonny Schneider for the first time. Back then he was a very well-known figure in trading. To say he was a character was an understatement. The meeting turned into an interview, if you can even call it that. It was short, five minutes max, and consisted of three simple questions: What's your favourite football team? If you could be any animal, what would you be? Do you like magic? He then proceeded to do a magic trick for me. That was it.

In another Ruffley twist, I'd gone to trade and then was somehow asked to run the entire trading floor. Sonny's brother was leaving the post and they needed someone, just like me it turns out, to run it.

I got to entertain some of London's top traders. We had seats at the Emirates Stadium, and I got to watch a good few Champions League matches. I met Peter Stringfellow while hosting traders at a champagne night at one of his new clubs. It was a dream job for anyone that liked to schmoose with a company credit card. I could probably write another book about all those stories.

Here's that word again: luck. As luck would have it, the only grad I knew to buy himself out of the Refco contract came to trade at Schneiders. We of course knew of each other, and he asked me to join his new team of traders.

I was mainly a Dax trader and he mostly traded the Euro Stoxx. This is the first time I'd seen someone (outside the risk room) trade that kind of size. Multiple 1,000-lot clips. Scalping the Bund, Bobl and Euro Stoxx. He really was an animal.

This is where I developed my averaging technique and learned to build up positions of size over short periods of time. Learning to take pain.

I was trading with decent size, consistently, and making money.

Be careful what you wish for. Being on the floor did have its disadvantages. The floor and the City life lost its appeal for me, as there was just too much noise and distraction. Having been surrounded by only other traders on and off the floor, I needed to be on my own. Focus on what I did, what I could go on to do, completely on my own. I decided to trade from home.

During this period, I funded myself as a trader. Shortly after I teamed up with this retail broker and ran their education programme while trading. I continued doing this as their chief market strategist for over a decade. I was now a pro trader, but trading in a retail environment.

I continued my trading journey, which had its ups and downs like everyone else, but endeavoured to keep my mission of increasing the size and speed I traded. Which I did. In spades.

While lots of my ideas and thoughts on trading were in my last book *The Ruff Guide to Trading*, which was published in 2015, a lot has changed in my life and the markets since that time.

I moved to New Zealand in 2017 not long after my last book. I now class myself as a pro retail trader. I have spent years perfecting my style of trading with three of my own defined trade types and two entry types. All combining my understanding of time and size. I still do this with a retail broker, which I will explain later in this book. Over that time, I have made close to six figures in a single day from trading. I don't do this every day, week or month, but when you make five figures in a few hours, four figures in minutes, you don't need to do it every day. That is how a pro and pro retail trader thinks.

INTRODUCTION

I'M GOING TO start with some tough love. You are probably never going to be a pro trader on the floor.

That's fine though. You don't have to be to make money from trading the markets.

A lot of time, effort and expense went into teaching me how to trade professionally. While there was huge emphasis on the theory of trading and the markets, there wasn't much preparation for what happened next.

Most of what I learnt about making money, and the profits that could be made from trading and trading with size, was done by making and losing money. Trading. Every day. Seeing first-hand what I could physically do in the markets and what I could achieve monetarily. It was a journey to understanding myself and my ability to trade in a way that suited me.

My professional style of trading size and averaging worked extremely well in the retail environment. Scaling (averaging) into positions allowed me to overcome the problems that retail traders will always face. Trading with a spread, slippage, speed of access to individual prices. Probably some more of that luck I will keep mentioning.

Pro and pro retail trading is about reaching a level of consistency. This may not be exactly what you think that means. The reason pro and pro retail traders make money is they have a balance. They trade and make money most days. They can make losses without losing momentum. They can also increase size when it is appropriate to do so and make bigger wins.

I think one of the biggest myths traders are sold is that you can easily make $1,000 a day trading. So, say there are 200 trading days a year, that's $200k a year of easy money. It doesn't work that way.

Trading is not that hard. People make trading hard. Making money, when you have sufficient capital, is not particularly hard. Keeping hold of the money you've made however, that can be very hard. Trading for a source of income and consistently making enough money to withdraw is the hardest part of all for all traders. Especially retail traders.

Trading is mostly all in your head. If you can understand yourself, get to a level where you can trust your gut, harness your emotions and recognise how the markets make you react, you are more than half the way there to making money as a trader.

From my extensive interactions with retail traders, one thing is clear. Retail traders believe learning more about certain aspects of trading will make them a better trader. This may be the case for some. However, being a better retail trader doesn't mean you will actually make money from trading.

There is so much trading education out there. If it's so good, why have the statistics on traders who don't make money retail trading not improved?

From my experience it's because retail traders who fail all do the same things. It's the retail traders who do things differently who are making the money. They are what I call pro retail traders.

I've made far more big trades as a pro retail trader than when I was on the floor. It's nothing to do with account size or environment. I want to explain what a pro trader is, what a retail trader is, why most people fail at trading and how there is a sweet spot where you can potentially be a pro retail trader like me.

This is my journey to making the amounts of money I've made in the last ten years. This is everything I have needed to know in order to do it.

1. WHO MAKES UP A MARKET?

THERE IS THE professional world of trading and there is that of retail trading.

While traders can trade most of the same markets, how they access those markets is fundamentally different. Professional traders have direct market access (DMA) and they trade directly with the exchanges. Retail traders do not. They trade with a retail broker which provides them with access to the markets via their own book and liquidity providers.

I will go into why this is important later.

There are lots of types and levels of professional traders from prop traders to institutional traders. While there are lots of retail traders, they really boil down to two types: those who make money and those who don't. If you look at the markets in their entirety, a large majority of the volume is dominated by the professional world. Retail only makes up a relatively small percentage.

You will often hear quotes like, '$4 trillion is traded every day in the FX markets.' That's big! I truly believe that most traders fail because they don't fully understand or appreciate big numbers. They don't think big enough. Looking back to when I very first started, I know I didn't fully comprehend how big the markets were.

Trading is like most things in life, those with the deepest pockets usually win eventually.

As a professional trader I had a lot of screen time. During this period there is a large element of sitting on your hands watching the markets. Not trading. I was waiting for something to happen. I traded volatility, I traded movement.

Learning where this volatility and movement come from is an important part of the job when you first start trading. It's less important now as I really don't care where the movement comes from. I'm not interested in being right and justifying why something is moving the markets, I just want to make money from it.

Trading is not investing, but the markets are made up of both traders and investors. This is where time and size are important. Pro traders do not hold trades longer than they have to. To a pro trader a tick is classed as one price movement. A lot is the minimum amount of trade size you can use. This can mean different things to the retail market of pips and points.

If you can understand why traders trade the way they do, for what outcome, for what reasons, the size, the time frames they hold trades, then you can start to understand how and why markets move the way they do.

Who has the most size? Who makes the most money? Who can move the markets with the press of a button?

UNDERSTANDING DIFFERENT TYPES OF TRADERS

Knowing more about the different types of traders may give you a bit more idea of how markets move. You have big institutional traders who have to trade huge size and hold positions to make their money. You have pro day traders who need to take their profits more quickly out of moves. You have retail traders who are just trying to jump on any movement.

This is why markets never just go up or down in a straight line. There are people trading different size, for different time periods, for different reasons. The aim is always to make money of course, and if you do it right you can make money out of any type of market movement.

Once you understand that the markets are just made up of people, it can be a little easier to quantify the fear and greed aspects of market movement. When you think about the average institutional and pro trader, then think about the average retail trader. When I did this it became a lot clearer to me why the markets seem to inflict so much pain on the traders who are least able to take it.

Ultimately, you have no control over the markets. You have to accept that. It's just worth giving it a bit of consideration so you know your place in the markets and the position of those who you will trade against.

Think of it as a pyramid. Institutional traders at the top with all the size and advantages of how they access the markets. Pro traders of different levels using their DMA and speed and screen time to trade off the big institutional money. Then the retail traders who have very little trading advantages at the bottom. Their main, maybe only, edge is understanding themselves as a person and trader and accepting the above.

The markets move because traders trade.

I'm going to start by explaining what a pro trader is. I have been a pro trader on the floor so I can do that. Other people who talk about the pro side of trading probably won't have done this. There are also the professional institutional traders. I'll then talk about retail traders. This really covers the attribute of all traders who have never consistently made money. I'll then talk about pro retail traders, which is what I am currently, and I would consider those small numbers of people who make money on the retail side to also be.

2. WHAT EVEN IS A PRO TRADER?

WHEN I REFER to a pro trader in this book, I will be referring to what I was. A backed pro trader on the floor.

You have two types of pro trader. Backed, by another trader or a house, or an own account trader, where you fund your trading capital yourself. Either way you don't get paid a salary. You pay yourself from the money you make.

The big difference between a pro trader and any other kind of trader who works in the professional world of trading is that one makes their own money to pay themselves, and the other trades other people's money, or institutional money. They get paid a wage, or earn fees and commissions, to do so.

Think about the charts and how you see the candlesticks being formed. After all, traders are literally market makers. Traders with enough size can move markets. It is very important when you are attempting to rationalise market movements that you take into account all of these types of professional traders.

Pro traders will want their money quickly. Institutional and professional traders of other types will want to push markets directionally. This in its most basic form is the difference between trading and investing. This is why you see short-term volatility, price action and market movement.

You must know and respect your enemy. Between them, the pros and the institutions make up a considerable amount of the total market volume.

You also have central bank involvement, and things like family offices and private equity. There is a substantial amount of money held by the hands of a select few. Not billions, but trillions.

Think about the pyramid. Who has the most funds and therefore the luxury to hold trades over a long period of time?

This is just a brief overview for you to think about. I have never been an institutional trader or a level of trader who gets paid to trade. I'm not going to talk about things in detail I don't have direct experience in. All the size and real money (paper) in the markets comes from the top.

PRO TRADERS

The first thing most people think about when you mention the word 'trader' is money. This is down to how the world of trading is generally portrayed and therefore perceived as a glamorous side of finance. It's all champagne and Ferraris.

I can confirm there is a certain element of that. I can also confirm that it's not like that for everyone, even for the pros.

As with every profession, there are those at the top, those in the middle and those at the bottom. There are different levels of pro trader. The bad news about this profession is that if you're not generating close to six figures a year then it's hard to justify being a pro trader. Which is also good news, as you're still doing OK in the grand scheme of things.

Pro traders backed or self-backed, with DMA, on the floor will need to pay trading costs and tax and then come out with a reasonable income. If you don't have an income from a profession, can you call it your profession?

My approximate set-up per month was:

1. Desk: £1,300
2. Bloomberg: £500
3. Eight screens: £300
4. TT licence: £250
5. CQG: £250.

Total: £2,600.

It doesn't really matter what the cost is now. It is a fixed cost you must pay. Let's just expect it's upwards of £25,000 a year if you want to trade on a floor. This was way back and some of the costs can be shared between traders.

If you're a backed trader, you may have to pay to get out of your contract. In my case this was £250,000.

There are of course those who make six figures in months, weeks, days, hours and, yes, even minutes. This is the bottom level of the professional trading world.

The middle level are pro traders who make seven figures, maybe eight. It's not for me to say if they are better traders, but they will be bigger size traders. I've met, managed and risk managed traders who have made these kinds of numbers on the floor.

There is only so much you can scale up before you move to the next level of trader.

At the top there are institutional traders, so traders who are professionals. These are the traders who can potentially make eight, nine, ten figures and more. Obviously, these traders who make the big money don't get to keep that money.

I don't want to overcomplicate something that is quite simple. There is a colossal amount of professional money in the markets. Everyone who trades has the same aim: to make money. How they do it, how they gain financially, is very different depending on where the money they trade comes from.

A pro trader may also trade products that retail traders probably won't. The main things that were traded on the floors were:

1. Bund
2. Bobl

3. Schatz
4. T Note
5. Gilt
6. Euribor
7. Oil
8. Euro Stoxx
9. Dax.

Pro traders trade a lot of interest rate related products, as that's what the banks and many institutional traders trade.

Traders on the floor were mainly scalpers. A scalp on the floor, in pro trading, is 1 tick or one price movement. When I talk about pro retail scalping this is just a very short-term trade, sub 15 minutes. This was in the days where you may wait an hour to get a fill in the Bund. There was a lot less liquidity across the board in those days. A lot of the older traders, who had come from the open outcry floor and pits did spreads, like butterflies and condors. I never got into these or attempted to trade this way.

PRO TRADERS AS PEOPLE

Here are a few points about pro traders as people:

1. Traders on the floor are mainly men. When I say mainly men, they were all men. On all the trading floors I have been on and in all the time I have spent with traders I've only met one woman trader. Is this important? I don't know. That's just a fact. Maybe it

has changed now? I would suspect it hasn't changed that much.

2. If you want to trade on the floor you have to be located near to one. In the UK that's London. The floors have got smaller from my day and there are fewer recruitment drives than when I first started. If you want to be a pro trader on the floor, your best and maybe only chance is to know someone on the floor. Meaning most of the people on the floors are mainly from the city.

3. Traders have an ego, traders have personality, but there is no noticeable edge in being the most intelligent person on the floor from my experience. I can say from meeting quants, literal rocket scientists who wanted to trade, they made the worst kind of pro trader. They were only interested in being right. They thought by being right in their calculations they would make the most money. They did not. In fact, they were more often than not spectacularly wrong.

4. The loudest trader was not always the worst trader, but they were never the best. There were talkers and screamers on the floor. I've seen screens smashed and literal fights. The quiet trader – that's the one making the biggest money.

5. You don't need to be on a floor to have DMA. Even back then you could have a DMA line to your home office. This is what the biggest traders did. They would come to the floor for big data events and when they wanted to be in the action. The floor served as a

unique place for making money when the conditions were right. Pro traders love attention.

You never got to meet or speak to the best traders on the floor. Unless you were friends with them. You never got to know what they were doing unless you were in their circle, or you worked behind the scenes.

I was, at any one time on the floor, in those circles or behind the scenes. However, as I found, too much time on the floor can be a negative thing. It's a boy's club and there are many professional and personal distractions to contend with. Spending your life around traders is not to be taken lightly.

My point is, the barriers to entry into the professional and the institutional trading world, by design, are quite high, probably too high for most people to obtain.

PRO TRADERS EXIST TO MAKE MONEY

There is a common theme throughout this book and a reason I keep referring to money. That's the ultimate and only aim of all pro traders. It was and still is the only reason I still trade. No pro trader I've ever met went into trading to make up the numbers.

Some traders were more subtle about the money side of trading than others. We all knew who the big traders were, and we all knew what amounts of money they made. There were the show-off traders who had all the things you'd expect: cars, watches, the trophy wife. They were the traders who wanted to make it known they were the ones making big money.

There were the traders who would be very discreet and very humble about the money they made, and what they spent it on. These were often the biggest traders on the floor.

Money is the leveller in trading. Few pro traders care that much about how they made their money. Pro traders see their very existence and purpose as solely to make money. It's where I got my, 'right at the right time' tag line from. It's all about making the money when it counts. How you did it just becomes a story, or if you're me, a book.

It doesn't change the fact that every trader on the floor wanted more. More money.

Traders are probably not who you think they are. Like any successful person, when you meet them, they are just ordinary blokes or women. But I can say that the successful people I've met do have something about them – they have *it*.

This *it* can mean a lot of different things, especially in trading. Not every trader has it and not everyone can learn how to have it. I have a level of it; I'm the Diet Coke of it. I had to create that quality for myself in trading terms.

This just means there are traders who make money from trading. A living. There are traders who make a substantial living from trading. There are those who kill it.

I'm firmly in the middle there, and I'm OK with that.

RETAIL TRADERS

This section is a bit longer. I feel that anyone who has failed to make money trading at any level does so because of some, or all, of the following reasons.

Firstly, retail trading is extremely hard. There are many factors stacked against retail traders making money.

If you trade via a retail broker or platform, you are a retail trader. It's that simple. Mistake number one, typically, is they will fund the account with money they *can afford to lose*. This is because this is what they are told. A simple way of reframing this is trading with an amount of money you *don't want to lose*.

This is a very simple mindset shift.

For example, a lot of retail traders will put a small amount of capital into their trading account, say $5k, to start. They will trade and invariably, due to that being some sort of test money, they will lose it. I have seen traders do this four, five times and more.

If you are serious about being a trader and making money, would you still have the same mindset if you put $20k–25k in at the start and only risked $5k of it?

Retail traders in my experience are usually underfunded when they start, overeducated (with the wrong kind of trading education) and have no real plan, or a plan that isn't suitable to their goals. Even worse, most have no goals at all, except they want a Lambo tomorrow. They are usually both unrealistic and underprepared as to what they can personally achieve. Again, most of this is not their fault. It comes from looking up trading on Google, or taking some generic overpriced course.

Remember, being taught how to trade is not the same as being taught how to make money from trading.

Time and time again there are the same things consistently being sold to retail traders. To avoid risk, trade small, place stops, learn *this strategy*. Pretty much the exact opposite of what I do.

I knew nothing of retail traders when I was a pro trader. I was surprised when I started speaking to them as to how many rules they had, and how overly complex their view on making money seemed to be.

I've dealt with thousands of retail traders via my webinars and my decade of being the head of education and chief market strategist of a broker. All of my education had to be approved by compliance so I could never explain in any detail how I traded and there was certainly no talk of how to make money.

I did however trade live and try to help traders any way I could, especially with my one-to-one mentoring. This book is the only way I know how to tell people how it's really done, by explaining all the things I have done and experienced.

I've long since said there are three types of retail traders:

1. Those who talk about trading and want to trade, but never put a trade on.

2. Those who trade without goals and any sort of plan. They make money but never keep hold of it.

3. Those who give trading a good try. Make and lose some money but constantly change their plan. They try to replicate past success, which never comes.

You would think there is a fourth type of retail trader in this list – those who do make money. That's true, but the rare ones who do make it are what I call the pro retail trader. I just don't think retail traders ever truly make it long term. Without the pro aspect the only retail traders who make good money are few and far between. They are simply trend-following short-term investors who got a single trade right and held it. Then they try to replicate that and almost always fail.

Here are the common traits of retail traders.

IMPOSTER SYNDROME

Basically put, feeling like a fraud, or that you don't deserve your success.

This is something that exists for people in high-profile professions and industries. Which trading is. However, I only class pro and pro retail trading as a profession – you can only call it your profession if you make a living from it. Retail trading is its own thing in my opinion. When I've dealt with retail traders there is a massive amount of initial enthusiasm: 'Let's give this a go!' Yet I often pick up that there is the inevitable fear of failure. Almost like it is predetermined subconsciously.

Retail traders for the most part when they start trading may think that it's something they could be good at, but secretly expect to fail at before they even start. There is always someone out there that is going to make the money, but it's probably not them. They are correct. That is the pros.

Either this, or they start making money and quickly begin to believe this is all by chance or simply down to luck. They believe this luck is going to run out, and once they start to think this way, it usually does.

However, to suffer from imposter syndrome, you must be at a level you feel is greater than your worth. In trading this is how much money you make, but if you have never made money, how can you be an imposter?

Trust me. You are not an imposter. You might make a few hundred, a few thousand, even tens of thousands. Name an amount. It will mean something to you, but the reality is that it's inconsequential to everyone else. When the FX markets alone trade $4 trillion in a day, as far as the markets are concerned, you don't even register. Remember, if you never keep hold of the money you may make, are you even a trader?

Most retail traders will never get to make the amounts of money needed to pay them back for their investment in themselves. Any success therefore feels like a failure. It's never enough reward for the time trading and capital risk involved.

You're not suffering from imposter syndrome; you are just experiencing the fear of the unknown. Which for retail traders is always to the downside, so the fear of losing money.

The pros don't fear the downside. They may only start to feel imposter syndrome when they are making too much money, which from an outsider's point of view is just the click of a button.

I've dealt with a lot of pro traders. Hand on heart, none had imposter syndrome. I know I've never had it.

Pro trading is hard. Not one single pro trader I've met thinks they didn't deserve the money they made. The pro trader's ego also won't allow it. You don't become a trader without having some form of ego. That same ego can lead to overconfidence, which can and does lead to losing money eventually. I can atone to that, but it's not the same thing. It's a different mindset or feeling completely.

Imposter syndrome for retail traders is just another convenient excuse, to justify them failing to make the levels of money needed to be a pro or pro retail trader. It's an idea usually presented to them via some form of education, which will then tell them how to fix it, for a small fee of course.

LUCK

I do believe an element of luck exists within anyone's trading journey. It's what you do with that luck, if you're lucky enough to get it, that counts.

If you can make good money from simply being there when the right trade presents itself, the momentum it gives you can be one of the most powerful things in trading.

Retail traders either through lack of experience or not knowing what a very profitable trade could look like, can rarely do it again. They don't get to experience the luck the pros do, because time outruns luck.

This comes back to the point I'll make over and over again. Pro traders have a career and if you stay in the game long enough, you will experience luck, and you might even create your own luck.

When you've traded for as long as I have, this sums it up:

> "The more I practice, the luckier I get."
> ***–Gary Player***

If you want to make money as a trader there can be very little practice, you should only play.

Luck as a trader can just be as simple as being sat there when things happen. I've traded many events and news opportunities. I've made big money (all relative) from them all. This is because I knew how to be 'right at the right time'. I knew how to make money. Once I'd done it I knew I could make more the next time there was another one. It's immeasurably easier to replicate making bigger money once you have done it.

Don't get me wrong. With every piece of luck, or what I considered to be luck, I could have always made more money in hindsight. I still always made good money though. I am not one of the great traders. I don't aspire or pretend to be. I'm at a level I am happy with.

From my experience retail traders just don't seem to hit the big trades when they can. All I know is, I have big trade stories, all pro traders I know have big trade stories, and very few retail traders have big trade stories.

THE MONEY ASPECT

I feel what retail traders need to get over are the practicalities – the physical and mental toll – of trading their own money. I always find the money aspect gets in the way far too often, far too early.

Here are some basics with regards to retail trading and trading your own money:

1. Never trade money you have borrowed, from any source. Ever.
2. Never expect to draw a regular wage from trading your account.
3. Retail trading should never be your only source of income at the very start.
4. Always know that no matter how disciplined you are, you can lose and will lose more than you wanted. Even if you use stops.
5. Making money doesn't feel the same as losing money.
6. You can never treat your capital as money you can afford to lose. It has to be treated as money you don't

want to lose. You have to put yourself in the correct mindset.

Everyone who trades wants to make money, that's obvious. They just want to make different amounts for different reasons. However, retail traders come at opposite ends of the spectrum.

Just as there are three types of retail traders, there are two types of traders that emerge when it comes to money:

- I need to make money.
- I want to make money.

Let's look at these now.

I NEED TO MAKE MONEY

Retail traders who need to make money to replace income, quit the 9–5 or want to do it full time are usually the first to fail. The pressures that come with giving yourself the goal of making a living from trading are just too much for most people. Even though they may have realistic goals, the reality of them meeting them in monetary terms is very unlikely in the short term.

The main reason for this is just real-world trading experience. Doing trades for the first time. You may have traded on a demo account or traded small size, but this is in no way, shape or form the same as trading real money to achieve real goals.

Whatever you did when it didn't matter will never be the same as doing it when it does matter.

The emotional side of trading is something that no one can teach you. You have to learn it for yourself. Unfortunately, the best way of doing this is by losing money. Nothing teaches you more about trading and yourself than losing money.

If you have to lose money in order to succeed as a trader, you tell me – how many people want to sign up to that?

People who need to make money are always on the back foot. Every loss of capital is not only money they have to make back, but money they are not potentially earning. It's an unproductive mindset to start with. Chasing a wage or trying to pay bills or simply exist off what you set out to make (which is usually unrealistic in the first place) is a lot of pressure.

I continually see the same pattern when it comes to people retail trading with the purpose of needing to make money:

1. Start out well and make some money. They are consistent with their trading size and duration of holding trades. Swings in the PnL are small. They take some profit out, though not as much as they wanted to take out.

2. The size of trades varies, and the size of losing trades starts to become greater than the size of winning trades.

3. The length of time holding trades increases dramatically. Winners are still small in comparison to losses.

4. They are left with a single trade with multiple positions, long or short, usually with a loss that is above 50% of their account value.
5. They accept the loss and stop trading, or they hold the trade as it's now at a loss they can't accept, which usually never goes the way they want it to.

I WANT TO MAKE MONEY

The traders who *want* to make money are usually in a very different mindset from those who *need* to make money. It's more that they would like to make money. They will usually be at a point in their life where they have made money in other ways and they see trading as another avenue to explore – the money makes money idea.

These traders are also on a spectrum. You have people who have made some money, in their other life, and now want that money to make more money in the markets (I call these people *entitled* traders). Then you have the opposite end of the spectrum of people who are financially secure and can fund a good-sized account, but don't ever really have any intention of doing what it takes to make money trading (I call these people *entertainment* traders).

WANT TO MAKE MONEY – ENTITLED

Some people think they can just come into the markets and throw money at it. Their trader life cycle is as I have explained above. They just have a good few noughts on the end. It very rarely seems like money is their main motivator, it's more about being right. I have seen this over and over again with people that I've mentored.

I've told people, sometimes just days before they do it, that if they approach the markets in the way they are proposing they will lose the lot. Which they did. They always go for a directional trade, they always add more into their *view*, and they have no other aim but proving themselves to be right. The only thing that happens is they prove to themselves they were actually wrong. Or in fairness they were right, but not at the right time. Who hasn't been there?

Generally, the money doesn't even factor into it. When they lose the attitude is, 'I can just put more money in.' They believe that they will win eventually.

WANT TO MAKE MONEY – ENTERTAINMENT

People who are financially secure almost don't want to make the money at all. They say they want to make money, but their actions don't stack up. They usually trade very small size compared to the account balance. They trade with very low risk and place very few trades. They are always in an evaluation holding pattern and building up to some big trade that never comes.

Again, it's another aspect of the mindset of trading that people rarely think about. If you don't *need* to make the money in the first place, why would you *want* to make it by trading?

My take is that in trading a lot of people really just want to be right. They don't always care about the money. Or more precisely, the money is a bonus. This is why the retail traders get a bad name. Trading is not a hobby or something to do for fun. It's a job, it's a way of life.

If you don't want to do what it takes, or don't want the money enough, then the chances are the markets will do their job and someone who does want it more than you will take your money.

This is why I respect pro traders. They have to make money to live off. It's not a game, a hobby or entertainment. I see it all too often, that retail traders think funding an account is *job done*. If you want to live off that capital you have to make money, build it, keep it, drawdown to live off it, and repeat.

This is what I do as a pro retail trader. The only difference is I trade with a retail broker.

This is why so many retail traders lose money or fail at trading. They may have the need to live off the money they say they will make, but they make the same mistakes over and over again and fail.

THE HOLY GRAIL OF TECHNICAL ANALYSIS

I come across many traders who fall into a learning black hole. They think if they know more, want it more and work harder, this will give them an edge to make it. More often than not this borders on obsession and gives people a form of trading *snow blindness*. They have *learnt* so much that everything starts to conflict. With so much knowledge of what should happen they can't deal with the reality when it does or doesn't happen exactly as they have been taught.

Again, learning how to trade, with technical analysis, is not the same as learning how to make money. I make no apologies for how many times I say that.

I've had people who have never even placed a demo trade tell me that they have read 20 books on trading. They have watched every video or webinar I've ever done. They have all this knowledge and theory and all they want to know now is, 'How do you trade Steve? What do you look at then, what do you do? What was the point?'

Everyone has access to pretty much the same information. We can all chart. We can all benefit and suffer from the self-fulfilling nature of technical analysis. There is no prize out there for being the best technical analyst, unless of course that is your paid job. Most of the best technical analysts don't trade and, if they do, they trade with very small size.

Searching for a guaranteed system simply doesn't work. At best you may get an 80% reliable strategy, as I do with Fibonacci. (This is a technical analysis tool I explained in detail in my last book, *The Ruff Guide to Trading*. It consists of retracements and expansions of moves between set highs and lows of specific points in the market.) To make money from the trade requires much more than just identifying something consistently on the charts.

Retail traders put far too much reliance on believing that if they understand technical analysis well enough, they can beat the markets.

I NEED TO UNDERSTAND EVERYTHING

This usually revolves around news and fundamentals. Reading the *FT* does not make you a trader. Not even close.

In my last book, I talked about the 80/20 rule of how the markets move in a technical and fundamental way. This is the area that has changed the most since my last book.

Retail traders, as with technical analysis, become almost obsessed with knowing more about the economy and the markets. You are not going to understand everything, ever. What's presented to retail traders in the form of news, analysis and valuable insights is mostly just a narrative set by the traders at the top.

Even if you could read between the narrative lines, it doesn't bring a lot to your edge in intraday trading. It may help with long-term trading or investing, but I don't know, that's not my area of expertise. What I do know is the markets don't follow the same fundamental cues the same way they did.

I have never known a time in my career as a trader where I discount news, even trusted sources like US data, as much as I do now. Quite frankly most of it is worthless from a traditional economic understanding.

There is a whole chapter on news and data, and how I read and interpret it, later in the book.

PRO RETAIL TRADER

I've made significantly more money as a pro retail trader than when I was a pro trader. I trade bigger size and I've simply been doing it for much longer.

I'm not going to tell you that you can be a pro retail trader by simply acting like a pro. It doesn't work like that. When I traded as a pro trader, I relied heavily on the speed of accessing individual prices. It was fastest finger first.

Having been a pro trader, when I started trading with a retail broker, my trading style didn't have to change much. It just had to literally spread out my entries. To start, I just averaged over more prices with less overall size. This is how I compensated for not having DMA. Later I added two more trade types.

It's not revolutionary. When people talk about a strategy, they want to know what strategy always works. None. It's a percentage game. By trading three specific types and two entry types, I get to trade a broad range of market conditions and if timed correctly have a greater percentage chance of therefore making money.

The main difference is I used what I'd learnt from the pro world. I had to personally push myself to keep increasing my size. Consciously keep making trades with bigger overall averages. I'd seen firsthand, in three different professional trading roles, that this is how the pro traders did it. How they made money. They may not have averaged as much as me, if at all – remember that the pros don't need to, they can clip much bigger size. The one main correlation between trading and making money from trading was the use of size.

I've met hundreds of pro traders in my life. Anyone can tell you what they think a pro trader is. I know what I know, because I was one.

A pro retail trader in its most basic form is a trader who makes money, consistently, with a retail broker. I know this because I am one. I know them, I have met them, sometimes as a result of mentoring them.

A pro retail trader may not be able to do exactly what a pro trader can do, but when the overall aim is to simply make money, consistently, over a long enough period of time, you will be closer to being pro in the most meaningful way possible. Pro retail trading is how you get to that point.

Everything in this book is how I now trade as a pro retail trader.

A FOURTH TYPE OF TRADER?

Having run a trading floor, there were certain rooms and places that even I was not allowed to enter. These rooms were the secretive domains of the black and grey box traders. I never really knew too much about what they did, except it was not for anyone else to know.

There has been a lot of talk recently about AI. I know for a fact that high frequency trading (HFT) and latency advantages the professionals use have been around since I first started.

There are a tremendous amount of automated trading systems in the market. I can physically see this in the price action of the markets I trade.

I'm no expert on AI, but if what we are told currently exists with AI capabilities, I'm 100% certain it has already been deployed in the markets. It's probably much greater than most traders, and all non-traders, care or dare to imagine, and someone somewhere I'm sure is making money from it. This will be the very top 1% of institutional traders, or at this point just another group of billionaires.

This is just another thing to think about, or not! When I think of my edge, how can I compete with that speed or level of money and investment? I can't. The only logical thing for me is to carry on doing what I'm doing and accept that the money I make is usually going to come from the retail traders in the market, meaning the pro element of pro retail trading will become ever more important.

You can never, and will never, know everything that's moving the markets. Don't even bother trying.

Trading is like a lot of things, like buying a house, investing for the future, etc. When should you have started? Probably yesterday. It's not going to get any easier in the future.

3. I KNOW WHO I AM

I'M A FAIRLY normal bloke originally from Bolton in the north-west of England. I've lived in a number of places in my life as a resident but ended up in New Zealand in 2017. A place I'd never been before I moved there. A Pisces, if that kind of thing interests you, married, one kid and two dogs.

Before I got married, I was a bit of a lone wolf. A digital nomad. I only existed in my own head and the markets. Maybe I didn't even exist at all? Important lesson there. There is more to life than simply making money. You need people important to you, to be around you and to have a 'life' outside of trading.

> "I spent a lot of money on booze, birds and fast cars. The rest I just squandered."
> ***–George Best***

As a person I'm generally on the pessimistic side, or as I see it, just a realist. I'm a pretty good cook. I don't like butter on sandwiches, which people just can't get their head around.

Handy to have in a quiz team. I know a lot of random stuff. I can also name most songs within three seconds of hearing them.

I don't like being told what to do. By anyone.

I have very few actual rules in life except don't be cruel to animals or mess with kids.

Knowing who you are and being able to identify your own personality traits is a key component in being successful at anything I have found. Certainly, in my trading. My EQ (emotional quotient/intelligence) defines me as a trader, much more than my IQ.

I have emotions, I'm only human. I'm not trying to pretend that those emotions don't come out in my life or my trading, they do. I see them as a tool that has to be controlled or harnessed.

I used to be motivated by buying *stuff*. That doesn't motivate me as much these days. I'm still motivated by making money, but now I have stuff. Like most things in life, I have found it was the anticipation of buying things that was exciting and motivating. Stuff is just stuff at the end of the day. It's also very easy to say, when you have lots of stuff.

Important note, however. Things and wanting to buy things is not always bad. It is a form of motivation to get to your goals. I have found I have needed to manage those goals and the subsequent motivation as I've become not only older but, dare I say, richer.

I won't do the Instagram trader thing, but yes, land, house, cars, custom Rolex... tick.

I never underestimate the power of motivation or momentum. No matter what that motivation is. Whatever gets me to that goal at that time, whatever keeps me going, that's what is important.

I came across this just as I was editing this part of the book on Twitter, now X and thought it was quite poignant to add.

> "Nobody is trying to fix the problems we have in this country. Everyone is trying to make enough money so the problems don't apply to them anymore."
> ***–Unknown***

This largely sums up where the world is right now for me.

What can I do? I can't change the world. I keep on trading, keep on making money. Isn't that all any of us can do?

It feels from the very rich, the famous, the powerful people down to the very poor, somehow, everyone is a victim of something. People keep looking to the government or some unknown entity to fix their problems. I don't, and never have thought that fix was coming for me.

The media and the narrative they have imposed on the world over the last few years is depressing. There is so much to fear. I have to constantly read between the lines and decide for myself what it is trying to achieve. This also goes for the fundamental side or the *financial news and information.*

Take the US economy presently (2024): everything is great in the stock markets and everything is positive! For now. Watch how fast and hard that narrative changes. Watch what happens in the markets.

This is why I trade. I will do this until I die. I have no plans or desire to ever retire from trading. I don't know a more time-efficient way of making money. Maybe drug dealing? Then I'm far too pretty to go to jail. I'd literally be passed around like currency.

I know exactly what type of trader I am.

From this short bio of me, I know who I am, but also how to interpret that into trader speak:

1. I'm pessimistic. Eighty per cent of my biggest trades have been shorts.
2. I don't like being told what to do. I don't use stop loss orders. I use my own monetary stops.
3. I moved to a country without ever having been there. Calculated risk taker.
4. I have rules. Though they are not overly complex.
5. I try not to follow the crowd or what the narrative says. I trade mostly within the trend.
6. I have emotions. I know what emotion to tap into to get the best out of myself in each trade type.
7. I trade as that's the best use of my time. I only trade to make money.

Let's get straight to the point here. I am an animal when it comes to trading. If you've read this book from the very start, you should be able to point out where that influence came from. I am my own person, my own trader, but I did take certain traits from others along the way. That's just human nature.

I trade significant size, relative to any account size, often at great speed. I trade averaged positions of 10 lots to 2,500 lots that last anywhere between two minutes (I have had plenty of sub-minute trades) to eight hours. I don't hold any long-term trades. Ever. I always trade using my leverage, and I have traded multiple accounts, sometimes simultaneously.

My technical analysis comes from my own proprietary software – iView Charts – which has featured on many of my webinars, interviews and live trades. It has not changed. It hasn't needed to. I use everything that is on the charts. I never overcomplicate them. I know more than enough about technical analysis to know I don't need anything new. Recent market moves may be more exaggerated, but they still chart in the same way. I trade on MT4, through a retail broker with Prime accounts.

My main technical indicator for trading entry and exit is still Fibonacci retracement and expansion levels. Again, there is plenty in my last book or free on my various recorded webinars to learn about that. Or you can get my iView charts that draw the Fibonaccis for you. Also, market correlations. Sometimes the trade I will take won't be in the market that is moving. Instead, I'll be looking at a market that could then move based on those correlations. A lot of the time I'm trading volatility and movement, certain types of movement that suit my trading style.

I trade at market, meaning I don't work orders; sometimes I just feel a buy or sell scalp, so I just hit the bid or the offer. I can just imagine the quants and technical traders rolling their eyes at the word *feel*. How do you quantify *feel*? You don't… and that's why I'll out-earn a quant intraday trader any day of the week.

Professional traders pay so that they can see the markets move. They pay to see the actual price movement. Access those prices. Why? So they can trade it and make money!

When scalping and trading correlations, moves can exist for seconds on the lower time frames to only then be absorbed by the charts. As a pro retail trader you are not trading the real markets! So what you see may not be what another trader even sees. You could call this price action or market flow trading. Again, not everything I do has to be pigeonholed or be a box-ticking exercise.

I trade what I see. I trade to make money, not to be proven right. They are two very different things.

I try to be market neutral where I can, which means I buy and sell short-term value with as little bias as possible. After being in the trading sphere for so long, this is probably still the thing I find most difficult to do. I have a bias in certain markets. Mainly the EU and euro are a failed social and economic experiment, so I *sell high* in the EUR/USD.

While that may limit some of my trades, I know my bias is there and I have to respect it.

I still only trade eight products, being the major USD FX pairs, the main indices and gold.

I've defined my trading into three trade types with two entry types. This has evolved from my pro days and has given me the ability to build a better understanding of how and when I take risk. It has also given me a way of breaking down how I need to deal with my emotions based upon the trade type and risk I then take.

I trade the news and economic data with a big pinch of salt these days. For the most part you should treat data events as *bonus trades*. As I'll mention, my biggest losses have been trading data. There will be a whole section on news, data and how it's presented to the market. No spoiler alert needed: how you read and interpret news is not how I do it.

When I do trade these events it's usually counter to my core strategy. If I perceive it to be sentiment changing, I will trade an averaged position with the aim of making relatively big money from that trade. Again, I can't stress this enough. Making big money from today's data moves requires a tremendous amount of risk.

As a professional trader you are paid to be the fastest finger over data and events. Even in professional terms I don't know how much edge this gives you anymore. For retail and pro retail traders this never really existed, and certainly in today's markets, it's just not even worth considering as any kind of edge.

HOW DID I GET TO WHERE I AM NOW?

I've spent the best part of two decades trading the markets or working in the trading world. My only other job outside of finance was briefly working as a greenskeeper as a student.

You know how I started trading. To get to where I am now, my journey, was a process of accepting the person I was at the time and applying my rules to the current market conditions. That might sound odd to you, I'm still the same personality type but I'm not the same person I was when I first became a pro trader.

> "A man who views the world the same at fifty as he did at twenty has wasted thirty years of his life."
> ***–Muhammad Ali***

As I'll continue to explain, to be successful at trading, it's mostly in your head. If you don't know yourself well enough, you will never be able to trust yourself fully enough to do the right trades at the right time and make money trading.

When you mention trading to the average person and ask them what it is, they say, charts, economics, maths, data, people with two phones furiously shouting. A lot of what people think they know about trading comes from films like *The Wolf of Wall Street*, and clips of traders on the news. It's all perception. Also, it's mostly wrong.

Take economics. I had to forcibly teach myself to forget a lot of it. Maybe forget is not the right word. I had to apply it less and filter out what was important and what was narrative. Most of the traditional economics, and how I traded it, has been blown out the water by QE to infinity and central banks doing 'whatever it takes' to fix the problems they themselves created. Inflation was the big one. At the time of writing this book it was seen to be an 'external factor' mainly down to Russia and the Ukrainian war. Nothing to do with every country around the world having the same domestic monetary policies of ultra-low rates and printing money like it was going out of fashion.

It's also important for me when I think about economic and fundamental trading that I factor in the time element. It takes a day, a week, months and years for things to filter into the markets. Very few things move the markets instantly. Unless they are unexpected, like an unannounced rate change, for example. Economics plays its part in investing and the markets as a whole, but for very short-term trading, the less I try and force a view on the market I trade, the clearer my trading becomes.

While people and traders move the markets, the tone and direction are set by the central banks, governments and that's filtered through the mainstream media (MSM) and news wires. Who do they take their instructions from? These days there are more questions than answers as to who actually runs the world.

It all boils down to a combination of instinct, experience and repetition. The accumulated trading experience I have from trading hundreds of thousands, probably, millions of lots.

I know my three trade types, and therefore what I can reasonably expect out of a trade. There are also two styles of entry, so in fact I have six trade types in total. Whether I'm scalping or positioning for the day, there is always a good amount of size and therefore risk. I have to be sure I'm willing to be fully committed, no matter how quick the thought process of the trade, otherwise what's the point?

I keep my clip size high. This way any trade I do, even an instinctive scalp, has size behind it. I do have to be careful of fat fingers though.

The two entry styles are based around a fade or follow scenario. It's pretty simple, I fade what I've seen, or I follow what I think I am going to see. Every trader out there knows it's a lot easier to put a trade with big size into what you have just seen, like a big spike, rather than what you may soon see, which is that big space of nothingness to the right. I place my trades off my charts, so the right-hand side is where the candles will form in the future, for anyone who's a non-trader.

I can say 'this is what I do'. I have rules, I follow a plan. I'm a disciplined trader. I can then instantly adapt elements of it. Within seconds I can be thousands of lots long or short. Why? I mean, it's not that I disregard it, it's more I have a trading instinct that has been crafted by years of trades. I have the ability to harness everything I know and turn that into a trade in milliseconds. I guess it's the equivalent of a trading muscle memory.

More often than not when I lose money trading it's because I hold trades for longer than I know I should. Time at this level and style of trading are extremely important factors.

It's an incredibly fine line that both pro and pro retailers like myself skate. This always comes down to speed, size and time in the markets. The less time I am in a scalp trade, the greater the chance I can get out for that good profit, small profit, small loss or break even. Once I pass the 5–15 minutes in a trade, in busy markets, I know the odds are getting bigger for me to take a loss.

This is why I have the three trade types. Why they have their own *set of rules* and time constraints.

The average retail trader in my experience has been conditioned to think that they must follow all the rules to be successful. Whose rules? I follow my rules. More than that, I do whatever it takes to make money. When you're getting out, I'm getting in. Where you're fearful, I'm brave. When you've had enough, I'm just getting started.

Putting on a big trade is easy, it's just the click of a button. When I say big size, it can be big compared to the account size I'm trading.

Managing the trade is the real art of trading. I can deal with the mental pressures of trading size by accepting why I put the trade on, no matter how quick or what my convictions or where I have been before. Also believing, trusting and drawing on the fact that my three trade types and entry style have worked more than they have failed.

What I feel has taken me to the next level to not only be able to put on the big trades and win but also be EQ aware. So, knowing how the markets make me react, how they push me and tap into my doubts and insecurities, which I still have to this day. How I harness my emotions and my ability to take short-term pain is how I make the money I do.

Repetition of entry style, repetition of exit, repetition of using my experience of the trade types. Harnessing the power of that familiar set of emotions. That's what pro traders do. That's what I do. That's what you should hope to achieve.

This is good as it keeps me alert and helps stop the complacency and arrogance that can come with big account trading, or indeed any trading. If you let your guard down for a minute the market will take your money and more.

I've done it and seen it happen to others more often than you can imagine.

No matter who you are, no matter how long you have traded, no matter if you even have your own risk team like I have! At some point there will be *that loss*. Anyone who says they have never lost more than they wanted to at some point trading is a liar.

Remember everyone makes money trading on a demo account. The difference between a big demo account and a big live account, or any sized account and making money, is simply the emotion we attach to it.

Before you start thinking it, stop.

Before we carry on I'll say it for you. 'It's OK for you Steve. You have traded big accounts, you can trade big size. You can make lots of money quickly, we are not that lucky.'

Luck. There is that word again.

I have traded fairly big accounts, but then again not that big, $300k USD, maybe a bit more at times. That is why I can do very large sizes, when I choose to. My biggest wins rarely come off my biggest sized trades, however. I also trade smaller accounts too.

I started trading small accounts just like everyone else. In fact, when you start as a backed trader you don't even have an account with money in it; you effectively have an overdraft. I spent most of my days scalping, with humble monetary fixed stops (even since day one I never used stop loss orders) building up my experience and momentum.

I wasn't handed money either. Like starting any business, you require capital, you find it where you can. I was backed by a trading firm, then another trader until I was in a position to trade the amounts and size I wanted for myself. I made connections, put myself in the right places with the right people, took relevant jobs to trading. Nothing in my early trading career was by accident; it was all by design.

When I came to be a pro retail trader, I considerably cut my costs. I approached it as my own business, but this time with my own money.

So going back to 'It's OK for you Steve'. I did my graft, I did the hard work to get myself into a position I could make the money I knew I was capable of. Over 20 years later I am where I am. You must be prepared to invest an amount of time in yourself if you take up trading. You can't be a victim of circumstance. You can't expect the world to simply hand you a trading career. If you think that it's always OK for someone else, you'll never make it as a trader or in life in general anyway.

You can still make a very good living by not being the best trader in the world. When you look at the money made globally trading, you could be near the bottom of the list and still be doing very well for yourself in monetary terms. I always aimed high. The key for me was to recognise I was never going to be the next Braveheart. That didn't mean I was a failure, it just meant I was being realistic.

HOW AM I DIFFERENT FROM YOU?

As a trader. Yes, I'm probably different, but that's the whole point of the book. I'm not promoting my trading style, more showing my middle finger to the trading education establishment, or the establishment in general. I make my own rules and trade how I want to trade.

We all have access to much of the same information, news, data and can trade on the same retail platforms with the same retail brokers.

I'm not telling you in any way, shape or form to trade like me. I'll be opening myself up, warts and all. Quite possibly to some harsh criticism and backlash from people who can't handle the brutal honesty of how to make money trading.

From my experience a lot of wannabe traders don't like the truth about success, what it takes or how it's really achieved.

It's much easier for them to immerse themselves in chat rooms or rant on social media, or take advice from people with no skin in the game but who promise them the keys to success, for a hefty fee of course.

Successful people in life take risks and do things differently from the herd.

The ability to be a free thinker and to trust yourself and your judgement is something that is increasingly being conditioned out of people in society.

If you want to be more like me, as a trader, then you have to pick out the key characteristics and attributes I demonstrate. You need to see if you can identify your differences, or similarities, and how you can use and incorporate them into your own trading.

I've made peace with who I am as a man and a trader.

I trade the biggest sizes when I feel the outcome has the highest probability of making money. They are not always my biggest winners, which is fine. I had to add more trade types to my trading to add a greater time element. Early on in my career I did suffer from elements of the *if only trader*. This means 'if only I had held this trade' or 'if only I had done that', I'd have made more money. This came from having a relatively big win very early on, only to then measure it against future trades. I then found myself trying to replicate that big win, which just wasn't possible or realistic.

It's easy to know that now and that was a small part of my trading journey. I knew I could make the big wins, but I didn't know how to consistently replicate it and was short-sighted in thinking only big wins mattered. Big wins being relative to the account size.

I typically will do lots of smaller sized scalps before I do a big scalp or large averaged day trade. The key is knowing when to use one of my three trade types. I know each of these instances instinctively. I understand myself, I trust myself and I do this day in day out. I am constantly leveraging my smaller frequent wins to allow me to attempt those big wins.

I believe I can identify at least one bigger trade at the very least every month, where I have the conviction to attack a trade with everything I have. Meaning I use as much of my size and leverage as much as I can.

I'll read your mind. When I trade small size, I usually win most of the time. Then the times I use big size, it usually loses. Lots.

That's what sets pro and pro retail traders apart from the retail traders. They understand one big trade can make you and set you up for the year or even life. Of the pro traders I've met over the years, which is a lot, they all have at least one *big win* story and I do mean all of them.

Size is all relative to the account you have, but at the end of the day the markets will move with or without the size I use. Even as a bigger pro retail trader you'll never move the actual market. You may move your broker's book and that is another thing to think about.

It's usually an instinctive trade with less thought of the consequences. When it's right, it's right. You just have to get as much into the trade as you can as quickly as you can. Then get out!

This is why so many retail traders fail. They think small, they trade small, and they lose small until they inevitably lose big.

I am not a retail trader.

Another thing I do differently from most people is I trade different trade types for different outcomes. I trade these on different accounts for different reasons. I trade different accounts in a variety of currencies, sometimes leverage. I'm always giving myself the slightest of advantages. Not always over the markets, I don't even know if that's a thing anymore, but certainly over other traders. I try not to chase the markets and let them come to me.

What I love about trading is that it is almost instant returns. The second I close out a winning trade my account size grows, and I can trade even more size. In the space of a few winning trades I can have the account balance and ability to do more than I previously could. It's like the compounding effect of investing, but in almost real time.

I want the money now, but have accepted that has been a journey to be able to achieve this. It took plenty of time to be able to *get rich quick*. I don't feel guilty for the money I make or how I then spend it.

I take my money out, I spend it. This makes it real. This makes trading real and a profession not simply a hobby.

What I do isn't that hard. It may be hard for you to comprehend it, and it may be certainly harder for you to put into practice. However, it's all just conditioning. I just keep doing what has worked in the past and keep doing it with bigger size when my previous trading performance allows it.

WHO ARE YOU? WHAT TYPE OF TRADER ARE YOU?

You tell me.

If at this point you haven't fully read, digested and pondered how and why I am the type of person, the type of trader I am, my question would be, how are you going to figure yourself out as a person and therefore a trader?

Have you even tried?

I don't read other people's trading books. I've never taken a non-professional trading course. I don't watch YouTube videos or watch TikTok, so I don't know what I don't know.

The whole point of this book is that I know what I know from all my experiences in trading, and here it is.

This is how I trade.

4. MY THREE TYPES OF TRADE

I'M GOING TO make an important point now. There is a lot of talk about trading strategies. The problem with a trading strategy is they don't always work. The markets change and the only constant in the markets is that they will continually change.

I am an expert in technical analysis. I am an expert in fundamental analysis, also narrative. A pro trader and a pro trader's strategy will be to make money from movement. Volatility.

While many elements of the above may go into a trading style, the trading strategy is always to make money. For this reason, I have trade types. I apply the trade types to the market conditions when I think that style of trade type and entry will have the best chance of making money.

Intraday, short-term trading is its own thing. It's not putting a trade on with a stop and trying to buy the low and sell the high. That is just very short-term investing, PnL watching, you win or you lose.

There is a lot to be said for trading within the trend. You can get good movement while directional trends form. There are opportunities when markets spike and break out of the current trends.

What I do is use my ability to put size into the market and get it out at a better price as quickly as possible, depending on how much profit I want to make and the time I want to spend in a trade.

The trade types I have are determined by time and how many times I can physically do these in a day or trading session.

My three trade types also have their own overall rules:

1. A scalp is a scalp. It can be an average, but only by definition, of multiple entries. It is not an *average trade*. You never hold a scalp trade for more than 15 minutes, so three 5-minute candles or one 15-minute candle. I have to be very cautious about turning a *scalp* into an *average trade* or *day trade*.

2. An average trade is held over a few hours, usually a max of three 1-hour candles. You can turn an average trade into a day trade but only if something fundamental or a major technical level break or event dictates.

3. A day trade is where I expect a market to close limit up or down. It will last up to eight hours, eight 1-hour candle closes. I don't hold trades for longer than this.

WHAT IS A SCALP?

The scalp is by far my favourite type of trade. There is nothing quite like hitting the button and banking more money in a few minutes than most people make in a few months. I make no apologies if this sounds arrogant to you. It's my job. It's what I do.

A scalp when I was a professional trader was 1 tick, one price movement. This is simply not possible to do as a retail or pro retail trader and you trade at market. Getting in and out of trades in a retail environment is a skill in itself. Especially when trading size.

For this reason, I am much more conscious of time and the monetary value of that scalp.

ONE OF MY MORE MEMORABLE SCALPS

When scalping I'm trying to spot the potential for a quick breakout or pull back. This is essentially the fade or follow entry in a nutshell. You would want to fade a spike and follow a directional breakout.

My rule is that with a scalp you're trying to take the most amount of money the market offers, the first time it offers it.

This may be the most important point I can make about taking any scalp trading with a retail broker.

Exactly what that means is when you have entered a trade and it goes *onside* you will be offered profit by the market.

Within that short period of time, it can only ever be so much, it's a finite amount. Money will be on offer, then it will not.

A true pro retail scalp will gain momentum and the profit from that trade will hit a profit point very quickly. There will be an amount of money, profit, you can physically take out before it starts to come back towards your entry.

The profits may go back up, but the profit can also all go and, in many cases, you can turn a winning trade into a losing trade by even slightly hesitating at this moment.

You have to take your money off the table the first time it is offered, at what you think the maximum profit may be.

What I have done is master this skill. I have a very simple *close all* button that exits all my open averaged positions when I choose to exit. My pro retail edge is that I can do this quickly, almost without thinking.

What you see on your retail trading PnL platform is not the real market; it is what you can see and what you can potentially take out from that position.

The time between what you see and when this can be closed may be subject to slippage. This can work for or against you. When scalping and exiting any trade in fast-moving markets there are no guarantees the price you are trying to hit will still be available in their market.

This is why speed of thinking and acting is critical.

Look at this logically and practically from all the points I have made so far about pro, pro retail and retail trading.

Pro traders:

1. Pay for DMA.
2. Trade the *real* market prices.
3. Scalp for 1 tick/price movement.
4. Trade bigger size.
5. Can trade in milliseconds and multiple times.

Pro retail traders:

1. Have no DMA; trade simulated markets.
2. Trade based on a broker's prices and liquidity providers.
3. Average to get the same *size*.
4. Have max clip set by broker.
5. Have time-restricted entry.

I average into positions to compensate for not having DMA. I know when I'm trading fast moves at market I will not always be price specific on my entries. I know that when I'm looking for a scalp in any market, I have to be able to get the size I want into the trade as quickly as I can on a retail basis.

I've done a lot of trades. I'm trying to keep these examples relative to today's markets. There was a FTSE scalp where the correlation between the FTSE, the Dax, Nasdaq and S&P were way out of line.

Correlations are just a way of measuring how markets move in relation to each other.

I have always had the same eight products set up on my trading screen, in a particular order to allow me to see what I believe the best correlations to be:

DAX ↓	GOLD ↑	S&P ↓	EUR/USD
NASDAQ ↓	FTSE ↑	GBP/USD	USD/JPY

The indices are broadly correlated, and in normal market conditions will generally trade all in the same direction.

Do you want to know how the professionals trade? They scalp a lot of the time based off chart or price movements. It is no more complicated than that.

I've put the practical points here for you to see, but there is a simplicity to a scalp, no matter what anyone tells you. If three markets are going down, in this case the Dax, the S&P and the Nasdaq, and the FTSE is going up, there is a very high probability that in the very short term the FTSE will go down too, and it does.

The only difference is I can trade the size I need to, when I see these opportunities and make some money from it.

How do I do this? Repetition. I've done this thousands of times.

Thought process:

1. Has there been any news or data out?
2. What levels have been rejected in Dax, the S&P and the Nasdaq?
3. Is there short-term value in a correlating market?
4. High probability scalp – fade entry (trading what I see).

5. Size.

Time taken: Approx. *10 seconds.*

Preparation:

1. Clip size increased to 85 lots (max 100).
2. Prepare to harness emotions.

Time taken: Approx. 5 *seconds.*

Emotion:

1. Controlled state of rage. This must be all or nothing, now!
2. Harness the fear. Can I get all my size in quickly enough?
3. Harness the greed. Can I get all this size out, onside?

Execution:

1. Entry at market towards Fibonacci level.
2. Enter as much size as I can, at market, 17 × 85 lot clips (1,445 lots).

Time taken: Approx. *15 seconds.*

I'll talk about DMA vs retail trading later. Putting more size into a trade requires you to just add more of the same clip size at market when trading to a bigger size total position. The max clip is 100 for the FTSE.

Trade management:

1. Are the correlated markets still going down?
2. Is the FTSE going down?

3. Is the trade on or offside after entry?
4. How much *open risk* did this cost?
5. What is the most profit this will show for a scalp fade?

Time taken: Approx. *90 seconds.*

Emotion:

1. Sorry you don't have time for too many emotions. They have to be rolled into the thought process and execution.
2. The fear and greed, which are the urgency to enter as much size as I can at a point in time. I can then exit the trade for a quick profit.

Trade management towards exit:

1. Once the trade goes onside this is purely a case of watching for patterns and movement in the PnL.
2. This was a very large position executed as quickly as it was possible on a retail platform. As the PnL went from four figures to five figures, I knew this was a solid return for what was only a few minutes in the markets.
3. Once the PnL jumped into five figures, which is why I look at the PnL not the charts, I press my *close all* button.

Exit:

1. Profit of approx. $11,000 USD showing.
2. Highly likely most profit showing first time.

3. Take money off the table.

Trade time: Approx. *2 minutes.*
Profit: Approx. $10,000.

That was on a $180,000 account.

That's a 5.5% return on a single trade, which is absolutely nothing groundbreaking at all in the trading world, at any level, at all.

The difference is that it was made in two minutes, and it was $10,000. In real-world terms, when applied to the normal rules and averages of how long it takes people to earn that kind of money from a job, then it becomes a bit more interesting to both traders and non-traders.

Now I've scalped too many times to mention. I, of course, would pick a good one to show. It doesn't make it the biggest or best scalp I've done. I don't have favourites when it comes to actual trades, just the trade types.

1. Do I trade that amount of size all the time? No.
2. Are the markets set up that way all the time? No.
3. Can I always be sure that the correlations will work? No.
4. Can I replicate that scalp trade again? Yes.

This was a truly instinctive trade that required me to go through the steps for a scalp trade very quickly. If I was trading a smaller sized account with smaller size, I would have done the exact same trade. Yet making $2,000 in two minutes, for example, which I have done, wouldn't have the same impact that I'm trying to convey.

A normal scalp fade entry, and I'm only calling it this as technically the market at the point of entry was going against me, really, it's just an *at market* trade. I had decided I was getting in regardless of what the market was telling me.

My *open risk* (covered later in Chapter 6) will vary on each trade. Since I always average – and especially when I average bigger size into positions – if the position is going against me, my PnL will go negative much more quickly due to this.

This may not be for long, as you are trying to get the pull backs from the extremes of the market move, but you can see a big jump in the amount you are *technically losing* just trying to put the trade on. This is why the time element in trading is so important to me.

This means I am putting more size into where I perceive the extreme of the move to be or simply the only prices I can get filled. When the market comes back the biggest size will be at the best price, which will then start to come into profit (or go onside) and cover my other trades. If I am correct on the trade, I can then net off the positions and close for a profit. This means closing all the trades at once, using the simple EA (expert advisor – MT4) *close all* button.

You can't use all your account margin and simply continue to buy/sell your way out of trouble. The old saying on the floor is 'if in trouble, double'. It's more complex but at the same time still quite simple. You have either predicted the extreme of that move in your entry and in that short space of time, or you haven't.

If you are wrong, then it's still the same process: *close all.*

I am trying to find an area of interest as to where the market will rethink. This can be a *fib line*, a level, a new higher high, it doesn't really matter. I am trying to find a place where the other traders (the types I have explained) may get out to allow there to be a short-term pull back where I can take my profit.

This means when you look at the charts and candles, you may only see this on the smaller time frames. The pull backs can be so quick that the candle may close at the high/low and it's almost as if it never really existed.

This is why retail traders gravitate to smaller time frames for scalps, the dreaded 1-minute chart or even worse *tick data*. This will not help you. It will only hinder you.

Trading as a retail pro trader you have to stick to the hourly, 15-minute and 5-minute charts. This is why you trade your PnL for exit. You have to trade what you see, what you can actually exit for.

Again – you are not trading the actual market. You are not DMA.

WHAT IS AN AVERAGE?

I always average into my entries. For the average trade it is a much less aggressive entry than the scalp. It is designed to space out the entry into an area of interest rather than any specific level.

I'm essentially buying time. Rather than having one entry with a stop, I have a number of prices that I identify as value and hold the trade for a longer period. The entry will usually be the same clip size for each one, and I will have an idea of how long the entry to the trade will take to put on. I will have a set amount as to what the overall size of the position will be.

ONE OF MY MORE MEMORABLE AVERAGE TRADES

This type of trade comes with its own set of emotions. I have to control those and accept this is not a scalp trade and be prepared to leave money on the table.

An example of this kind of trade is where I made $77,000 in two hours from a 40 lot gold trade on a $30,000 account. That's a 256% gain. This was 4 × 10 lot entries.

To me that's turning a relatively small account into a big account. That trade was not even that big in lot size, but the size of the trade was relatively big for the account and from a margin perspective. It was simply a *being right at the right time trade.*

I don't usually increase the clip size of the average in this type of trade. I pick a position clip amount relative to the account and factor in the ultimate overall position size I want to take. This will mean putting the same clip size on for each entry into the average.

These trades are less reactionary and therefore you have more ability to go through the thought process. Generally, as you will be in the trade for much longer than a scalp, every part can take less time. This doesn't mean it is less stressful than a scalp or require less emotional harnessing.

For me these trades are more stressful and harder for me to make the most of. I have to both harness and control my emotions.

I've traded big news events numerous times. From terror attacks to the introduction of QE to wars. I've done very well from trading events. This event was Russia declaring war, or invading, Ukraine, you choose the narrative take on that.

Once again, I take no pleasure in these events; this is just my job. To know how the markets and how the other traders, of all types, will react to this news. I then trade accordingly.

Thought process:

1. In the MSM, war is indicated to be imminent.
2. What is Twitter (X) saying?
3. What are the more credible news sources saying?
4. How are the markets correlating?
5. What is the market saying about risk? Stocks in risky situations usually go down. Gold is a safe haven, usually goes up.
6. Five minutes after the first report I read "Nothing is happening".

Time taken: Approx. *5 minutes.*

Preparation:

1. Trade the best account of the news.
2. Clip size adjusted to maximum overall position I can take with that account.
3. Prepare to harness emotions.

Time taken: Approx. *2 minutes.*

Emotions:

1. Harness the fear. Is this the end of the world as we know it? Is it real?
2. Harness the greed. This type of trade has made me big money before. Do not miss it when it goes.
3. Control the anxiety. Why is nothing happening immediately?

Execution:

1. Entry at market.
2. 4 × 10 lots, essentially max out leverage and margin.
3. Entries close together as you just don't know how fast the market will react.

Time taken: Approx. *5 minutes.*

Trade management:

1. What are the correlations doing?
2. Is gold going up (as I'd suspect)?
3. Are the indices going down (as I'd suspect)?
4. How much open risk did this cost?

5. How much have I made before from similar size and events?
6. Time. Is this still an average trade or do I turn it into a day trade?

Time taken: Approx. *2 hours.*

Emotions:

1. Control the frustration. Why is this limit not up? Why is it not moving faster?
2. Control the doubt. Is this really the right trade to take? You're a pessimistic person, a bear, so sell indices?

Trade management towards exit:

1. Once you see big numbers it's hard not to take them. I'm very time focused when I'm in any trade.
2. Once I'd decided that this was not a day trade, then it's simply looking for a technical level or PnL amount that is worthy of taking.
3. From experience you can get big pull backs, so at this point am I willing to take 10–20% drawdown to get 10–20% more at this point? No. It was enough money for me at that point in time.

Time taken: Approx. *2 hours.*

Exit:

1. Profit of $80,000 showing.
2. Close all.

Trade time: Approx. *2 hours.*
Profit: Approx. $77,000.

That trade was on a $30,000 account and was a 256% gain. Is that enough for an end-of-the-world trade? Possibly not, but if it really was the end of the world, would money matter anyway?

When you have traded and seen as much as I have in the markets, you can't take yourself too seriously.

For events and news like this you have to put yourself in a higher state of consciousness. It became very quickly an all-or-nothing trade. This is a mindset trick. The max downside risk was $30,000, which in the grand scheme of things is nothing. It was a trade opportunity that was almost guaranteed to make money at some point very soon. The risk, you just had to take.

This is the pro and pro retail trader attitude to risk. It's all to gain not just what you may potentially lose. No one can ever take that trade away from me. It could have been more, it could have been less. I could have cut it out for a loss. I didn't though. I was *right at the right time*. I did what I had to do in that situation. Make money.

There are lots of things to consider about these types of trade.

Mine was an average trade entry but I had to handle some of the emotions differently. I have a wealth of experience of having traded big events before, but I also have all the other emotions which I find hard to harness and need to control. This all goes back to *I know who I am. I know what kind of trader I am.*

The emotions I find hard are frustration and doubt.

The frustration is from not making that quick money. Obviously compared to a scalp that has more trade entries and more size added as the position builds, profit comes quicker. So it's recognising that frustration and controlling it rather, and then harnessing it.

I know that events and shifts in sentiment will move the market in a certain direction. How much? You never really know. Especially since the world, and to some extent the markets, has become so desensitised to news and even wars.

This is why I set monetary goals and assign cash amounts to stops and profit targets. I make it real for me. I had hoped my trade would be a six-figure trade, but from seeing the PnL movement and my time old rule of not leaving money on the table, I decided: 'Don't be a prick for a tick.'

The doubt, or disbelief that something big is actually happening is something you have to come to terms with as a trader. You know, as much as you can with anything in the world today, that this is *real*. You have to then both control the doubt and harness the past experience you have with this emotion. Remember that making good money is your job, it's not your fault.

I could always have made more, but what was good for me? Where did that amount of money stack up in my overall daily, weekly, monthly or yearly goals? It was a very good profit for that period of trading.

At heart I was trained, and still am, predominantly as a scalper. This trading style appeals to me as I like to take money out the markets fast. Once I've made up my mind in trading and most things in life, I have little to no doubt of my convictions. I know myself well enough that if I dwell on things, I can talk myself out of what was the obvious answer. Which is always my first answer. Well, 99/100. With big decisions and trades I'm not often wrong.

The doubt emotions or feelings were easier to manage with this average trade as this was an event. A sentiment-changing piece of information. I've traded these before. I know what I've done in these situations before.

For many traders out there this was a big trade that didn't take that long. For me as a trader everything over 15 minutes in a trade is a long time.

Time vs money. It's what I live by when trading.

WHAT IS A DAY TRADE?

A day trade is where you enter a position or series of positions to allow the maximum amount of time for a trade to run. I class eight hours as a day trade. I don't hold trades for any longer than that.

ONE OF MY MORE MEMORABLE DAY TRADES

I've made $90,000 from a $120,000 account, a 75% gain. That was a 700 lot Nasdaq and 60 lot EUR/USD trade that ran for about eight hours.

This was a technical trade based on levels and sentiment. The Fed was rapidly hiking interest rates and the language had turned more and more hawkish, meaning rates were likely to rise further. It was one of those *feel* trades that required size and time. I had to let the markets reward me for putting in the size and making the conscious decision to hold a day trade.

Trading off a fundamental view is extremely dangerous. It is great, as you have seen from my gold trade, when it is *new news*, even if some of that news has been priced into the markets.

However, convincing yourself you know what will happen based on a fundamental view, or more importantly a narrative that has been purposely set for you, is very precarious these days. I have a lot more to say on the MSM and narrative in trading later.

I was going against the trend in the Nasdaq, as stocks have generally gone up. I was also breaking my rule, or bias, of buying the EUR.

There was an element of *buy the rumour sell the fact*. There was also a bit of conflict on the correlations of rates going up and buying the EUR, so essentially selling the USD.

This all comes down to how I read and interpret news and also how I trade based upon a narrative filter. No one knows what the markets are really going to do. On a long enough time scale we can all spot which direction a market will eventually go and where it may get to. Again, that's not how I trade. I trade the in-between volatility for short periods.

I started with a Nasdaq short then averaged into the EUR long shortly after. The levels in both looked good and had some good trading momentum results behind me, so this was the reason for the size and trading a day trade, which is not something I do all the time.

With both a day trade and an average trade most of the hard part is to put the position on. Especially when trading two products. I wasn't hedging the position. I don't do that. It was just a way to average out the size of the overall position.

The first thing certain types of people, be them a trader or not, will say:

1. What prices did I enter?
2. What technical indicators did I use?
3. What else were you looking at?

The whole point of writing this book and writing it in the way I am, is that you are not me. You will never be me.

You need to get past the point where you think making money is down to solely using a trading strategy. Making money in anything is doing the right thing at the right time. Using your account to make the most amounts of money you can is the level you need to get to, not simply a level of technical or fundamental understanding.

This is why I make the amounts I do from trades. I know what I look for. Any level of trader should be confident enough to know what to look for. The difference is I have done it. I still do it. I do what I need to do from a time and size perspective when it comes to trading.

In this instance I wanted to make money. I had good momentum behind me. I wanted to put a good-sized trade on that I was willing to hold and watch the trade for up to eight hours. That is trading. I was at the extremes of the markets for entry. This was a follow entry style trade. I didn't know what levels would be hit, but I knew the levels. I knew if I got a good average and the trade on side it was one that could run. You have to manage your expectations and the trade from that point.

You could call it a swing trade. You could say it was a key reversal. It was just a good trade. You can back test your strategy all you want. Nothing, and I do mean nothing, works all the time.

Thought process:

1. Fed language?
2. What does that language mean to retail traders – narrative?
3. What does that language mean to pro traders – interpretation?
4. What does that language mean to me – how do I trade this?
5. Is this new news, priced in or moving the markets?
6. What is the direction of the main USD pairs telling me?
7. What is the direction of gold telling me?
8. Indices go up on pretty much any news or bounce from the lows.

9. Is this going to be a day trade opportunity or just an average trade?

Time taken: Approx. 30 *minutes.*

Preparation:

1. Check the correlations. USD/JPY, gold, eye on indices.
2. Less aggressive clip size (EUR) and entry will be averaged over a few prices into areas of interest. Max lot on the Nasdaq as it's quite cheap in comparison.

Time taken: Approx. *10 minutes.*

Emotions:

1. Control the doubt. Is this a day trade or an average?
2. Manage the greed. I don't put day trades on that often compared with other trade types.
3. Fear. The fear is that I get rewarded by taking short-term pain. This is not a scalp, this is a longer-term trade (for me).

Execution:

1. Entry at market
2. 7 × 100 lots Nasdaq, 6 × 10 lots EUR/USD.

Time taken: Approx. 25 *minutes.*

Trade management:

1. The first part is to try to get your trade onside. Trying to establish that you have made the correct averaged entry. This means assessing the risk for the first stage of the trade.

2. As I trade big size, taking averages on when the market goes against you is expensive.
3. Once the risk starts to come, to break even is the hard part. All my emotions then come back into play.
4. Fear, doubt and greed.
5. Managing the onside part of a day trade is the hardest thing for me to do, perhaps in trading. Why I don't do it that often.
6. I have to set levels and be aware of my monetary goals for the week and month, even yearly.
7. The absolute key thing to take into account is the previous loss. In order for this not to be a revenge trade, it can't simply be a size trade to get even.
8. Most losses I get back with scalps and averages over a period of time. The fact I am putting on a day trade means it's based on what I see to be a big move, and something I can make money from.
9. When the trade is onside I'm watching the PnL. I'm watching how fast it decreases, but more importantly the increments by which it increases. In good trade your PnL will jump quicker and not come back as fast.
10. You can obviously see this in the candles, but from a scalper's perspective I'm always conscious of how the numbers move.

Time taken: Approx. *7 hours.*

Emotions:

1. Control the frustration. Why is it not going faster? Easy – it's a day trade Steve!
2. Harness the greed.
3. Manage my expectations. I hate spending more time in trades than I need to, but this is a day trade. Time has to become my friend and not my enemy.

Trade management towards exit:

1. Very much in the same way as I did with the average trade, at a point in time there is a slowing of the PnL. The jumps have stopped.
2. Eight hours is a long time in a trade.
3. Could I have put in a stop? Yes. Could I have put a trailing stop in? Yes.
4. Have I done my job, did I make a good amount of money? Yes.
5. Know when enough is enough for you.

Time taken: Approx. *7 hours.*

Exit:

1. Profit of $93,000 showing.
2. Close all.

Trade time: Approx. *8 hours.*
Profit: Approx. $90,000.

What I do in these three trade types may not be that groundbreaking to you. News flash! I know it's not. There is very little new in trading. The secret, whether you like it or not, is to trade big when you have the opportunity. Know what trade type to put on and when the market conditions favour you and your trading style and personality.

Most traders are just looking for permission to trust themselves. That trust has to come from within you.

I risk money to make money. That's all I think about when I'm trading. The money.

It's not about if I'm going to be proved right by the technicals, the fundamentals, the *plan*. Yes, the money comes with being right to some extent, and having a style, but it's the fact that I do the same things, over and over again. I trade in a way that allows me to function within the markets I choose to trade.

It's not overly glamorous. It's not that exciting, but it works for me.

I trade by my own rules, and therefore decide when and how I want to bend or break them.

Retail traders have been conditioned to believe they have to have all these rules to be allowed to trade their own money. It's your money. If you don't respect it, you will lose it, or more accurately another trader, like me, will take it from you.

Successful people in life don't seem to play by *the rules*; they play by their own rules.

5. TWO ENTRY TYPES: THE FADE AND THE FOLLOW

THE FADE

A FADE IS WHEN you do the opposite of what the market is showing you. Simply put, if it's a big green candle you sell it.

My entry into a fade trade, like all my trades, will always be averaged. Meaning I trade at market and will enter multiple positions to take an 'averaged' position in the markets.

I do this because one price on a retail broker's platform, to me, is meaningless. I want to spread out my size into an area of interest. I don't want the perfect entry price, as if I do, I've already missed the bulk of the trade opportunity.

If you're a swing trader, traditional day trader or investor this will confuse you.

Pro retail trading is much more about getting some meat out of the move rather than picking a top or a bottom. We all know bottom pickers get smelly fingers by the way!

I said right at the start of the book you will have probably traded based on this type of movement, and probably lost money. This is because it is very visual and by design drags retail traders into a market. Sometimes, apparently, for no reason.

There is always a reason.

The reasons this happens are:

1. Markets move and people make money. Simple.
2. Low volume markets are easy to manipulate.
3. Stops can be triggered very easily.
4. The best way to maximise the money made in a trend is to break that trend in the short term.
5. In high volume markets, momentum can greatly exaggerate trends and directional moves.

Think about the types of traders I mentioned, think about the size and way they trade and hold positions. Short-term spikes will benefit the very quick short-term traders and the longer-term traders. They are designed to stop out and take the money from the average day trader. The traders who *risk 1–2% of capital on each position* type of trader. The ones that follow the rules that *they* say you should follow.

When I see these types of moves there will always be one of my three trade types I can use. It will invariably, mostly, be the scalp.

If I'd only ever placed scalp trades in my career and I'd not had the momentum that comes with big average and day trade wins, I don't think I'd be where I am now.

There are various factors that I always take into consideration when seeing this type of move. They offer a high probability for success if they are taken for what they are. For the majority of the time it's part of a bigger picture move by traders who have more capital and time than I do.

This type of movement can be the reason for a trade in some cases. This is what makes it so dangerous. You are trading what you see. This is where years of experience and knowing what has happened to markets in the past is invaluable.

Obviously it goes without saying, you do not have to try to fade every large move or candle.

When I see this type of movement the first thing I check is the obvious one. The correlation between other markets. Then the news. A lot of the time this type of move will be seen in only one market. Usually something like gold.

Gold is priced in USD so I check the USD/JPY: gold goes up, USD should go down. Gold goes up, (safe haven) indices should go down. New news, data events, all markets should really move if it's changed the overall market sentiment. Basic thought process.

When it happens in only one market, that is the time to consider if it is a big enough move to shake out weak short or long positions. Does it have the potential to retrace some, all, or create a complete Fibonacci expansion scenario?

This is a lot to think about, especially when a lot of the time these moves, by design, catch you off guard.

Essentially if you are trading what you see, you have to expect, not the unexpected in my view, but the completely obvious. Pain. Short-term trading pain is coming.

The more the market shows you, if you are not already in that move, the less you should always expect to get out of the trade. This is why I trade size and make every pip count.

This suits my personality type and also my main trade type, the scalp. There is a caveat, however.

TYPES OF FADE ENTRY

SCALP FADE ENTRY

This is where it gets harder. This is where my *plan*, my trade types and ability to think quickly really come into play.

It is very important, critical, when I trade a fade entry scalp that I decide right there and then whether it is a scalp or an average trade. If it's a scalp, then the clip size is bigger. I have to make a profit (or be willing to break even or take a small loss) the first time there is a pull back in the move.

This means the trade can only win or lose (I don't see a breakeven as a loss, I also don't see many breakeven offers with this type of trade).

These days I will always try to scalp rather than average. That's just where I am in my life.

The average trade entry, the same size clips and building into a position, does give you a greater chance of holding the trade longer.

I'm always buying or selling towards a level or a point on the chart that the markets will retrace. This means I want to be entering at the high/low of the candle as it approaches my key levels. This again can be a Fibonacci level, a higher time frame level, whatever is on my charts. Remember my charts for all the products I trade are already set up. There is no confusion as to where the market may go, just my judgement as to how it will get there, and crucially when.

You can't simply jump into a fade; it doesn't matter how big the candle is. It is much more important to see how the market gets to where it will go. In this way I am trying to predict where I think the market will get to, as that's what everyone else also looks for, but I factor in the *pain* element.

I'm trying to trade to levels, even though I know these levels logically will be the target and may possibly be broken in the short term. It's back to that idea of an area of interest. Who knows what levels are really set in stone? It's all just judgement. A point in time.

Sounds hard, right? It is.

The whole point is trying to catch the extreme of the move, to enter at prices that will form the eventual high or low of the candle I'm trading. When the market turns, that should be where my biggest size is filled.

Most of the time I will be trading towards the close of a 5-minute candle, so when the next candle opens, if I have judged the move correctly, and averaged the right amount of size over the right amount of prices, I would already be filled towards the extremes. I would then be looking for the next candle to be opening below the last position I entered.

This type of entry is all about predicting the short-term future. If you do it with big size you have all the same emotions you have with any scalp. Your PnL can decrease very quickly and you can easily lose money as these are fast-moving markets, and the majority of your size will be at what you perceive to be the extreme but may not be.

With most things in trading, if it were as easy as seeing a large candle and doing the opposite, everyone would do it.

The key points are to get into the trade as late as you can, but not too late that you can't take advantage of increasing your position into the extreme. The whole point of this is that when the market hits the extreme it will always pull back, but to what extent? Who knows? Each trade and move is different. The way I make money this way is taking that movement and adding into the trade in a way that when the pull back comes, no matter how small, it will be relative to the size of the move. More often than not, if you've done all the seemingly impossible stuff above, then you make money.

Also, I almost always take the profit the first time it is offered. A lot of the times, with big moves, they have to retrace, but then they carry on in the direction of the move. This is why a scalp is a scalp is a scalp. If you try to turn this into an average trade, you will lose that ability to make a quick profit. It doesn't mean the trade won't turn out to be a good one, but you have entered into it as a scalp, so the risk of a secondary move, when you are carrying that size, means the risk is much higher.

AVERAGE FADE ENTRY

Most of the same principles as the scalp apply to an average fade entry. As I said at the very start, I will have decided if this is a scalp or an average. If this is an average I will be much less aggressive on the clip size of the entries and also will usually not increase it for each position.

This means I can build up into an area of interest and take less overall risk, compared to a scalp. It also means I can *leave money on the table*. I'm not looking to take profit the first time it is offered.

When markets spike, they then consolidate towards the extreme. It will stay there for enough time to make traders either side of the trade doubt their conviction.

I trade the averaged position with a fade entry often when there has been new news, data or an event. This means that if it has a potential to change the sentiment of the market there is more chance of a serious retracement. In these cases all markets should move accordingly, not just one market.

People can say what they like about market manipulation; it happens. What can you do? This is why if one market moves, I will usually scalp. Maybe other people will interpret those moves differently. It was certainly different when I wrote my last book. There is just too much highly concentrated capital out there to know for sure now.

When multiple markets move, an average trade is a better option. If all markets are correlating and moving, this gives me more confidence to look at a bigger money, longer-term average trade type.

You can turn a scalp into an average position, but the initial retracement has to be severe, so severe that you never go back offside. This happens, but not that often.

You can turn an average trade into a day trade. This depends on the reason the trade was taken in the first place. For this reason, there is no real day trade fade entry that I've ever taken away.

SUMMARY OF FADE ENTRY

When you are scalping you are trying to identify when the first major pull back will be. It may not pull back for very long. This is why you have to take profit the first time it is offered. If it is not, you have to take a loss. More than likely the move, if it doesn't have a significant retracement, will continue in the direction it is going in the short term.

For example, you can see a 50 pip green candle retrace 50% for four of those five minutes, by the close of the candle if it's closed at the top. Those 25 pips were available for a very short period of time, minutes, in some cases seconds. When the candle closes, it's like they never existed at all!

If you are averaging into a position, you are trying to catch the extreme of the whole move, not simply when it has its first retracement where the actual high or low of the move closes.

THE FOLLOW

The follow entry just means you are trading to the right of the screen. Into the unknown. You follow the market to where it is going to go. A potentially vastly more profitable way to trade versus fading what you see. In some ways this is much harder to do.

Predicting which direction and where a market will eventually go is pretty easy. Visualising how it will get there and what that movement will look like is a lot harder than people think.

Unlike the fade where you have a strong visual cue, there will usually not be a lot happening in the markets. You will usually see a tight range. You can use Bollinger bands or trend lines, channels, to show you this, but it should be obvious the candles will just be smaller.

The follow entry can be good for a breakout scalp. Again, you have to be aware that when a market initially breaks the range or starts a directional move, there will be an initial pull back at some point. This is where taking the maximum profit the first time it is offered has to be balanced out. When following the trend you may get a better max profit than that of a fade entry.

Also, it is much harder, I find anyway, to average positively into a trade. When I'm trading this way I keep my clip size high and just try to get as much of the same size into my overall averaged position as quickly as I can. This is a skill in itself. It's much easier to add increasing size as a market is spiking against me than to add size into the unknown.

The entry style of a follow entry scalp is very much the same as an average position.

I have to choose what it is before the trade. I can choose this in the trade management of the trade, but if I do, it's usually too late to take the initial profit. So by default this becomes an average trade.

This has caused me problems. Obviously when a market breaks out there is an element of quick movement, which I like. It's very rare that a market breaks out and goes exactly where you think it will. I've certainly had big scalp wins, bigger than you ever think possible when you put the trade on. They are rare, however. Most of the time the real move starts much later on.

This is why you need to decide the trade type. A good follow entry scalp will not be as profitable as a good follow entry average trade. This is why a scalp can last for up to 15 minutes. I'm much more likely to hold a follow entry scalp for 15 minutes, but the fade entry scalps are usually less.

On balance the follow entry does yield more consistent returns. They are easier to manage from a size and risk perspective as I don't increase the size of the clip, just add to the overall position size.

All my years of trading have simply come down to a combination of size and time in the trade. Having three trade types and two entries just simplify what I can do. The simpler it is the more I can replicate it.

6. RISK

You can't make money trading without taking risk. It's as simple as that. There is a balance between taking risk to make money and managing risk to protect your capital.

When any trader first starts out, they ideally should use stops. They should keep their stops tight in monetary terms, but I'm not talking about starting out. I don't read other traders' books, but I see a lot of the same comments and remarks on social media regarding risk. Mainly, risking 1–2% of capital on each trade.

It all revolves around a retail level of risk and knowledge. This is fine, but these people have not seemingly experienced the professional world of trading to the extent I have, if at all. I have a pro trader attitude to risk, which always reminds me of this quote:

> "There are old traders, there are bold traders, but there are very few old, bold traders."
> ***–Ed Seykota***

The number of times I trade, and the entry types I use, can only be done for certain amounts of time by design. There is only so much you can do in a trade. There are only so many trades to be taken in a day. If you over-trade and try to push too much from your account, there is only one inevitable outcome.

I take risk and short-term pain while trading fast-moving markets. I take a lot of risk when I think the most probable outcome is making money, not being right on the overall direction of the market. I'm a trader, I'm not an investor.

Being great at trading is more than making great trades. Being good at entry styles is much more important than picking the perfect entry point. Trust me, watching lots of pip movements over time doesn't compare to making lots of money from less pip movement in short amounts of time.

I see risk in both time and a monetary value. Of course, I'm trying to be right and win trades, but I don't use my capital and risk experience to buy the low and sell the high. The money I make is down to the trade type and applying the entry style to the market conditions that they give the best probable edge to.

Taking more offside risk doesn't mean you'll make more money. That's not how trading works. Simply letting a trade run offside and holding it isn't a skill or something any level of trader should practise.

The main difference with a pro trader and a retail trader is that a pro will be holding a bigger offside risk because some sentiment shifting has hit the markets: a news event, or something that the markets have not yet priced in. They won't be holding a big offside position because they can't accept the loss. They have a risk team to do that for them. In the pro world there are only *own account* traders that can take excessive offside risk.

Have I seen a pro trader do this? Yes.

I've seen a €250,000 offside print turn to a €500,000 onside print in a day. I spoke to the trader when he was down this amount. We discussed the trade and that was that. As it was his money, there was only the hard stop of what was in his account. It was close. Speaking to him afterwards about whether he would do it again, he said, "No, well not until the next time."

Have I seen a retail trader do this? Yes.

I've had a retail trader tell me he doesn't want to hold positions anymore and wants to try to scalp. He then went on holiday and left a position open, with no stop, shorting the market (USD/JPY). This lost close to six figures in a few days. I asked why he did this and he just said, this time it felt different.

A retail trader will hold a trade because of the fear of losing their capital over their conviction about what's happening. They get to a critical point where the loss is emotionally too much to take. They are left in the situation where it is better to hope the position comes back closer to their entry and take a smaller loss. That is a more preferable, or in most cases the only, option to taking that size of loss. At this point they are rarely thinking about a breakeven and certainly not of making a big profit. They are mainly just wanting to get out for less of a loss. I'm not saying they always lose, but they certainly don't win that often from these kinds of positions.

What separates the pro in terms of big risk is that they can make the big money on the other side. It's rare to see this in the retail world. Anything is theoretically possible in trading. My whole attitude to risk, trading and life is you simply don't know what is possible until you do it for yourself. Also, you have to take your own responsibility for your own actions, win or lose

As a pro retail trader, have I done this? Yes.

I have taken too much risk at certain points in time. I have placed a lot of trades. My biggest losses have been from holding trades around data announcements. I have had a couple of significant losses over the time I've traded where I believed the market had to do what I thought it should do, based on what was announced. The times I've taken more risk were when the accounts I was trading were up, most of which were up over 100% or more in profit. Still, these losses were in the tens of thousands of dollars. It was sentiment-changing data and I had a good reason and understanding behind the trade to take on the risk. I took on more risk in terms of time and was expecting a big return for that risk. I have had no problem ever closing out a trade for a loss. When you convince yourself, no matter what, that you are right. This is when the market often teaches you the harshest lessons.

Any trader who hasn't had a loss, a bigger loss than they wanted to take, or taken on more risk than they had wanted to at some point in their career, is either the single best trader (I've never met) or they are lying.

As I've said, all pro and most pro retail traders have a big win story. Invariably there is also a big loss story.

My whole attitude to risk from where I am now, a pro retail trader, is that I risk the most on the actual entry. The average and the entry are where most of my initial risk sits. If the entry average is good, then I should be taking an acceptable risk (for me) at that time. This again will depend on the trade type and the time that allows it to be held.

It's about time. I don't want to spend any more time offside than I have to.

I take more risk than is deemed acceptable in the retail environment. I admit that. I want to make money from all my trade types. That comes down to time and entry. The risk I take is based on the experience I have of trading all my trade types multiple times. That's the best way I have found with regards to taking risk and making money from trading.

My main point with risk is that there is a massive gulf between those who can take risk and get big rewards, and those who take risk who have never made it pay. If you have never made money from risk, or made significant wins from trading in general, you need to approach your own risk much more cautiously.

PRO RISK

From my time on the floors and trading pro this is what I've picked up. Pro traders don't have that negative *risk is bad* mindset. I know I've said it before. This is important.

I've explained that professional traders have a risk team behind them, they have an approximate monetary amount they can lose in a day or session, there is some tolerance, but it's limited. I can assure you it is never 1–2% of their account.

When you trade professionally the mentality is it's never over until it's over.

You can trade in the morning and lose money, take a break, trade and make it all back and more in the afternoon. If you don't you are simply stopped out for an amount and can't trade until the next day.

The idea of risk and risk management is to take the emotions (usually of a loss) and to some extent the decisions away from traders. In reality for the trader, they are made to stop trading before it ever gets too unrecoverable. Having that impartial voice that can tell you 'that's enough for now' is something no retail or even pro retail trader will ever get to experience.

You have to do it for yourself.

Having been a professional risk manager, it comes down to the size of account, the trader's style, reputation, experience and track record. It's also having the benefit of seeing not only what the markets are doing at that point in time but seeing what the other traders are doing. That's invaluable for any risk manager. When you've watched hundreds of traders' accounts, simultaneously for 10 hours a day, you pick up patterns.

Almost all pro traders I've encountered wanted the maximum size they were allowed, if not more.

A lot of the time spent professional trading is just covering the costs. Scalping. Being in and out the markets for small pip wins. Not to be confused with small amount wins. It's the better trade opportunities that make professional traders the majority of money or profit in a trading year. It's a business, traders know that over time the opportunities will come. This really sets them apart from retail traders. This is the mindset the pro retail trader needs to be in when looking at their own risk profile.

On the floor I'd never spoken to any other pro trader in terms of risk–reward ratios. I'd never spoken to any other pro trader about what they did when they lost money. We just didn't talk about risk or the negative side of trading in that way. You would acknowledge the bad days and the only option, which didn't need to be spoken about, was to carry on and make the loss back.

How you chose to do this was down to you. If the risk team did its job correctly then the loss was usually manageable.

Most traders talked in pip term gains rather than money. This was a respect thing among the pros. Everyone would eventually find out the amounts as pro traders are notorious gossips. You knew who the traders were around you and their reputation, so you kind of knew the amounts that would be involved anyway.

A pro trader's risk was a discussion with each individual trader and the risk department. So I know more about this than most other pros. My discussions were again mainly about size limits and the positives of what they would do in scenarios where they could use them. I can't stress enough how much of a positive view traders have of the potential upside or risk and size rather than the downside risk of losing money.

I set and enforce stopped for many pro traders. Some big ones. I've stopped out plenty of traders. I've had every discussion, argument, disagreement and almost punch up, every scenario you can imagine. This is because a pro trader has to think they are almost always right. They know they are not, but being able to blame the risk department for stopping them out was just better for their egos.

'If you hadn't stopped me out that trade I would have won.' We can all say that.

This external risk influence the pros have is a massive edge over both pro retail traders and retail traders. Pro traders will hate to admit it, but they know this to be true.

Trading at speed and with size is an incredibly hard thing to do. It's a skill most people will never even know exists let alone aspire to do.

If you were hoping I have some magical insight into pro risk from my days as a pro trader and a risk manager, sorry once again.

As a pro trader (unless you are own account) your stop is set outside of your control by the risk department. You stop trading when you hit that monetary amount. If not, you are physically stopped out of all trades, outside your control, by the house.

Pro traders take risk but it's still within the confines of their account and house limitations.

That's it. Pro trading is much more black and white than most people realise.

Acknowledgement to all people on the other side of the floor. Risk management is the least glamorous most underappreciated job in pro trading.

RETAIL RISK

I've talked to a lot of retail traders, many more than pro traders. I do hear the occasional big win story from retail traders, but more likely than not it's just a trade they have managed to hold directionally. The majority of retail traders who have a big win story, 99% of the time this is then eventually followed by a big loss story. Then, no more stories.

As a retail trader, or especially now you should be thinking in pro retail trading terms, you have to be both a trader and a risk manager. This is both confusing, conflicting and hard to master.

I've said it before, and I'll say it again. One trade can make you, but one trade should never break you.

The reality for retail traders is they never make enough from holding the best opportunities. They take too many big losses from the opportunities that just turned out to be bad trades, made worse by holding trades or moving stops.

The thing I see time and time again is that retail traders hit a negative monetary amount where suddenly the outcome doesn't seem to matter anymore. They have lost so much they can't see a way back. If you remember when I spoke about the pro trader attitude, it's not over until it's over. This is a key difference between the attitudes to both risk and eventually wining, at any cost, in trading.

Risk is risk and it should be down to you to understand from your trade types what is a reasonable risk to take on each trade. Risk should also be a combination of where you are in your trading journey and where you are in relation to your monetary goals. If you want to use 1–2% of your capital on each position, that's your call. From my experience, it's death by a thousand cuts.

Retail traders will want to talk in terms of risk–reward ratios, which is sensible for investing and longer-term trading. It's not as useful in short-term trading and especially not in averaging or scalping. If I trade an averaged position there is no way I can keep to a 1–2% risk. Especially in a retail environment.

The problem is that retail traders want to be told what to do with many aspects of trading, especially with risk. They want guarantees, assurances. They want to know what works. I'm afraid making money from trading doesn't always allow you that luxury, especially when trading for short periods of time. People can tell you what they have done, like myself, but what you should do? It's really down to you.

Trade more, lose some trades, win some trades and learn. See what you are capable of achieving. You will never know what you are capable of until you try it for yourself.

Momentum, which I will get to at the end of the book. This is one of the most underrated things in trading, period. For most retail traders, the story is all too predictable. Their attitude to risk is usually contrary to that of the pros. The emotions of losing money are just too overpowering to cut losses. The fear and greed I use and harness for speed and urgency are translated into the opposite of holding trades for longer periods of time. While this can work in your favour, it can work much faster against you. The whole process of risk is never approached in the right way from the start.

Much of this is because of the plan that most retail traders have failed to implement. They don't know what a profitable trade looks like in risk parameters personal to them. All the risk is to the down side and the desire to make money is overpowered by the emotions of losing money.

They learn risk from what they are told, which as I've said with most things trading, there is no one size fits all! I truly believe the rules in trading, business and to some extent life, are meant to keep people firmly in the average category. Success, money, power and control are for someone else not you when following the rules.

MY PRO RETAIL RISK

I've had to balance what I observed in the risk department, the trading floor and what I've personally achieved while pro trading and pro retail trading. For me personally I've always talked in terms of money when I'm approaching my pro retail risk. I've explained how my motivations work. I risk in monetary amounts and time amounts.

I had to find out what my own risk style was in this environment. Although I had more experience than most regarding risk, I was still at heart a trader and I wanted to make money. I've had to wear both hats at the same time, like all pro retail and retail traders will have to do.

I no longer had anyone in the risk department watching.

Increasing size and therefore making increased amounts of money is just a mental trick. You have to look at hundreds like tens, thousands like hundreds and tens of thousands like thousands. They are just numbers. The number can be expressed as a percentage of account size. You can look at it as pips. It doesn't really matter what it is as long as it works for you.

I swore to myself that having seen the pro, been a pro and seen what the top traders did from being in the risk department, I could only ever get to the level I wanted to be by mastering trading size and the risk that came with that.

I'm only ever trading three trade types with two possible entry styles. The majority of my trading really consists of two trade types and one entry style. I have done these trades thousands of times. I know the numbers; they are ingrained in me. This is where you need to get to with your risk.

I've done so many trades. As a pro retail trader I've had to accept that the retail cost of trading has to be included in my risk. I've accepted that the way I average has its own cost that has to be included in my risk. More cost/time based risk on the entry type. This means I can't work to small risk parameters. I'm working anywhere between 1–20% risk on each trade, but only for very short periods of time at those higher levels: minutes and seconds.

Open risk (no stop) being offside for seconds and minutes is not the same as risk with a stop. The open risk principle only works with a fade entry and generally on a scalp trade.

My risk is not simply letting a trade go offside and hope it comes back. That is not trading, that is just hoping. That is PnL watching, leaving yourself at the mercy of the markets and time. My risk is getting as much size into the entry as the trade allows. Negative averaging will always require higher risk, even if the trade is a high probability risk. Positive averaging will require less risk, but it is harder to trade the overall size I want. It's all a balance.

My risk is set by monetary amount stops and time. I've tried to make it as simple and clear for me to follow for my own benefit. Every trader has rules for a reason. If you break them, in some ways even if you profit you have already lost.

SCALP: FADE ENTRY RISK

Risk varies between my three trade types and entries. For scalping, especially when negative averaging, I talk about *open risk*. That's just the term I use. If I'm trading a fast-moving market and doing a fade entry scalp, I know it's going to cost me more money to put that trade type on. However, I consider the open risk to be more of a time factor than simply just a monetary factor.

It's important to remember that with big account sizes you may be able to put more into trades, but if the average is entered too early you can't simply buy/sell your way out of trouble.

The majority of this risk is taken by physically averaging over a number of prices to get the averaged trade position.

The idea of having a trade on for most people is you have your entry, a stop loss and a profit target. That's how they measure their risk.

I'm trading into moves that may retrace for seconds or minutes and that open risk is what I am trading and basing my risk on. The risk is based on the size and speed of the move. The more you see the less you get an opportunity to get that first real pull back.

People don't like that. People don't like hearing it or accepting it as it doesn't fit in with what they have been told to do.

Open risk only works with this type of trade and entry. Although I don't use a stop with other trades either, they have a fixed momentary stop in my head.

Open risk is something I have to calculate quickly. It means I have to decide how aggressively to increase the size of the clips and where the biggest size will be towards the extreme of the move. This is why I wait until the normal price action of the spike, which will catch out most retail traders, starts to increase size and open risk to get to my levels where I believe the market will offer that first pull back.

So once again, a lot of this depends on having the technical side of the trade ready on my charts. I then need to average at the right level and position the biggest size all very quickly to then allow the pull back to occur and then to *close all* when the PnL shows a profit for the first time.

If I've explained the scalp fade entry trade well enough, you would see why this risk approach makes sense. It's impossible to trade this way with the risk profile of how most retail traders trade. A lot of the risk in the trade is in fact the actual cost (spread) of putting the trade on that way.

If I were to put a fade scalp on a small account, for example, I would enter a trade with an initial 1 lot, knowing that the averaged amount would be 12 lots in total:

1 Lot
2 Lot
3 Lot
6 Lot

12 Lot total

Since I can at times trade much bigger sizes (the maximum being 100 lot clips) I'll start with a 40 or 80 clips trade and enter multiple times at prices as I average. It will always be more than the initial entry amount but doesn't always have to double in sequence.

As the trade goes against me (which I always expect it to do, almost encourage it) I am buying or selling into levels or points of attraction. I can chart as well as anyone. Any level, any point of attraction is just a line on the screen. I'm a very visual trader, so I'm paying attention to how the market gets to these levels and areas. The speed, the way the candles are formed, with an averaged entry I can choose where to enter my size. I want to get the most size at the extreme of the move. This can often be when a level is actually broken, but I have to start somewhere. This means invariably that if I'm right on the trade, my smaller initial entries will always go offside.

This will sound counterintuitive to most traders. Why put trades on that you know will lose? Why not just put all your size at the top or bottom?

Simply, I don't know where the top or bottom will be. When you do the same with bigger size, due to the maximum lot size limit I've explained with a retail broker, you can't even get that size off. This is the best way I've found to enter trades of size, any size, on a retail platform, that is to manually average in over several prices with higher increments of size.

I'm making split-second decisions to add more to the trade, to see if there is a pull back, to take profit if it is offered or to simply exit the trade for a loss. This all comes down to huge amounts of time spent viewing charts and trading on a retail platform. Even if you work orders, you can't guarantee to get fills. In fast-moving markets you can't guarantee anything. This is why the pros pay for DMA.

My trading style has been constantly refined to suit the retail trading environment. To me these are always high probability trades. I know the more I see the less I will get from the trade in pip movement as a retracement, especially the first significant retracement, which is where your profit should be on offer for that first time.

By the time I've entered my biggest size the market should already be coming back in my favour. This is why the *open risk* lets me deal with the fact I'm risking a lot in conventional retail risk terms, but it should only be for very small amounts of time.

Once the trade comes back, the bigger size is covering the small entry positions and I'll be waiting for the market to come back to my initial entry and take that max profit when it is offered for the first time.

You need to have the ability to mentally hold a lot of factors in your head. Visualise your trade in real time in your almost trading consciousness. This again I don't know how to teach or explain better.

RISK-REWARD RATIO

Another favourite term retail traders love is risk–reward ratio. This is because it is quantifiable. It has its place in trading, I don't deny that, but this applies mostly when you are trading over longer periods of time.

I'm only interested in making money. As are most pro traders. When you eventually trade big enough size and make every pip count, this is where making money becomes a reality. While a retail trader may use a 1:2 risk reward, risking $50 to make $100, no one, and I do mean no one, cares. Not even you if you're being honest.

The amount of size you put into a trade is when the risk vs reward has true meaning. When you're risking thousands to make thousands, that is when trading becomes more interesting.

I'm happy taking 1:1 or 2:1, 3:1 and more, negative risk ratios. Risking $2,000 to make $2,000 or $10,000 to make $5,000. This is because of the time element. It can be minutes or seconds that I'm showing an offside position and most of the time that last jump in the negative PnL is because I'm putting my biggest size in at the extreme of the move. It costs money to put that size on and a few pips movement when the entire position if offside looks worse than it is. This is why I refer to it as open risk. There is no stop to realise that loss.

I understand that people will find this approach hard to get their head around. There is no other way of entering size when a trade is going against you.

IS IT THE RIGHT SPIKE?

I said right at the beginning of this book that you may not know what a fade entry is, but you will probably have traded one.

When I'm scalping I'm always looking for a low risk trade just like everyone else. I just do it in the opposite way. I look to put my size into the market and get less of a move with more size, knowing that the trade itself is what should make the money, not the market direction.

It may be a high capital risk trade, but if the average is correct and the timing is correct the trade itself is not a high probability risk trade. It also has to be the right type of movement. One of my key skills is that I know which spike to fade and which to leave alone.

The markets over time will go from the highs to the lows and vice versa. They never get there in a straight line. There is always profit taking and pull backs. That's where I make my money. Most of the time when I'm exiting a trade you will only see that movement on the smaller time frames as they get swallowed up in the higher time frames.

I know what speed, direction and feel of move I trade well. This is all from trading these types of moves for decades. It's the ability to take my fundamental view, analyse the technicals and trade my averages in a very short space of time. After enough time, trading becomes instinctive.

A lot of my attitude to risk when trading this way is based on the move itself. This trade type and entry I've done countless times. I know what I have to do. The moves are all unique in their own way, but spotting the right spike for the right reasons means the entry and risk will usually happen in similar ways, only the time in the trade will vary.

SCALP: FOLLOW ENTRY RISK

This type of risk is less risky in nature as you are essentially going with the trend. This way I will add to the trade as it is going onside or into profit. This can be referred to as positive averaging. Breakouts can happen fast, so it can be hard to get size into that type of trade.

The initial risk for this trade can be low. Sometimes you take as close to zero risk as you can get in trading. Once you enter the trade it can go immediately onside. The problem is, as I'm used to multiple entries, how quickly should I start to average? If I start with a set clip size the trade can move and the ability to add can be lost. As it is a scalp, which has its own time constraints, I can find that I have to do these entries a number of times as the trend continues to make the money I would have done with a bigger average. This can mean taking a loss on some trades while the market continues to break.

This can be frustrating.

The risk for this trade is probably suited more to conventional risk attitudes. I will usually start with a higher clip as, if the move allows, I'll be putting more of the same size clip into that trade. As I am trying to catch the actual breakout and not be simply positioned before, I may want to hit the market several times. This will depend on the size of the account I am trading due to max lot limits. Even when trading smaller accounts, I will still prefer multiple entries over one single clip.

In reality, the fade scalp entry lends itself to adding to trades better as it is much more reactionary, so it really resonates with the fear and greed, the sense of urgency. I've had to train myself to add multiple entries at the same price or levels to get the same results from a follow entry. For whatever reason, the emotions and how fast I can react to a fade entry are not the same as a follow entry.

You can't be a master of every part of trading. I've still had some very big wins from this style of entry. I'm just pointing out that nothing is ever 100% straightforward when scalping, even though in theory it should be the easiest trade to do.

RISK-REWARD

The idea of a risk–reward ratio does work better for this type of trade. As I have the same clip size for all entries I have an idea from the start of how much the trade has cost to place and any offside risk I've taken. As the market is breaking out in one direction (that I'm trading with) I will know fairly quickly the risk I've taken, unlike the fade entry where open risk can be much higher as I am going against the markets aggressively for very short periods of time.

I work in monetary terms. So for illustration, I will usually aim for at least a 1:1 risk–reward ratio. Usually it could be

1:2 or 1:3 depending on how aggressive the breakout is. This also depends on whether I'm taking the profit the first time it is offered, as it's very, very unlikely it will be the max for that move.

This is the big difference with going against the trend and going with the trend. If I'm trading very well, I will get out for profit and then get back into the trade again. This is the perfect trading scenario. Banking profit and then trading again to catch more of the move. I'd love to say that I can do that all the time, but I can't. It's actually very difficult to do consistently.

If I have caught the right breakout point, the market should move generally in five waves:

1. initial breakout
2. pull back (of any size)
3. continuation
4. consolidation
5. continuation.

These moves happen quickly, so you need to be adding to the average in the first initial breakout candle. A big breakout can move a great number of pips in a matter of seconds or minutes. Much like the fade entry rules of taking your profit at the max, the first time it is offered, the follow entry is the same.

If you look at any big breakout on the smaller time frames you will see the initial breakout, then a quick pull back, then the move continues, then stops towards the low/high for some consolidation before continuing in the same direction as the breakout.

This of course needs to be a significant breakout for that to be possible. The speed you have to get in and out is just as quick as the fade entry exit. This is why I have the *close all* button.

There is also the risk, while we are talking about risk, of not taking the profit the first time it is offered and looking for the five-wave pattern to continue over more time, to make more money from the trade. This happens a lot. There are patterns in movement even before the candles on the time frames I trade close.

This is where you can decide to let the trade run longer or turn it into an average trade. It usually plays out just the same way as the five waves. If I'm waiting for that to be displayed in candles, I may be waiting for 15 minutes (three 5-minute candles). This is always a judgement call and one where, if conflicting as it has so many similarities to the fade trade that I know, I can bank quick money. However, if it's so similar to the average trade entry style, I always think, could this be a much more profitable trade?

IS THIS THE RIGHT BREAKOUT?

Breakouts can happen after a period of consolidation, on news, data or a key break of a technical level or trend.

The key thing I always look for is the speed and size of the move. The quicker the movement happens the more likely other short-term traders will be wrong, leading them to liquidate positions. This will add to the move.

Like most things in trading, you can overcomplicate these things. Anyone, even a non-trader, can spot a breakout happening. You have to base your risk on your understanding of the nature of the breakout:

1. Range breakout – you've been waiting, but so has everyone else.
2. News – is it new news, big news?
3. Data – narrative, what was the market expecting?
4. Technical – how significant is the break to the overall picture?

AVERAGE/DAY TRADE RISK

Most of the risk aspects of an average trade and day trade are the same. The types of entry I have explained in the scalp entry.

Most of what I'm doing when assessing risk is really around my entry. If I'm not looking to take profits out quickly and accepting that I will be leaving money on the table, then the risk and then reward just comes down to time.

I know I've used the word *time* a lot in this book. It's up there with *size* and *money*. There is a reason those three words appear so often in this book and my trading philosophy.

If you want to make real money trading, like the pros do, like I do, you will have to place risk and use size when the opportunity calls for it. Being right, at the right time.

I know most traders will not want to hear this, mainly because you know deep down you will never be able to do it.

My $77,000 gold trade win.

This required $7,000 risk, so 23% of $30,000. In retail risk terms, from what the experts tell you, this is too much. This is why I make money and they do not.

I'm going to break this down into how a pro and a pro retail trader think and why that risk is acceptable, and why I do these trades when I do:

1. Open risk. I'm not using a stop. So there is risk and a cost of putting that trade on. What's the exact risk? You don't know, you never know. It's expensive to trade gold in the first place. It's always going to cost money, each 10 lot entry costs money to place. That's not risk, that's a cost of trading.
2. I average into prices. This trade from my initial entry went offside, negative, so I did a fade entry and negatively averaged at better prices.
3. I was 99% sure I knew what gold would do on this news. It would go up. It had nothing to do with the overall risk profile of an average. It was a trade type I'd done before. It was an event type trade I'd traded before.

4. So gold was going up, there was nothing more certain, or as certain as any trader can ever be on anything. So at what point do you get in? Right away. You never know how quickly the market sentiment will change and what size and trader types will enter the market. This is trading.

5. There was no question that I wanted to put all the size that account would allow. I did 4 × 10 lots. The max margin that account would allow.

6. The $7/8,000 max downside PnL print was for about 30 seconds. The PnL can vary at the extremes for milliseconds, so it's hard to pinpoint an exact amount. That $1,000 is a big percentage movement in *risk* terms of 23% to 27%. In that 30 seconds the open risk, if it had a stop, or a monetary stop, would have meant the trade would have been stopped out.

   The trade remained offside for about five minutes in total. It went from $7,000 to $5,000 to $2,000 very quickly. I'll ask again, is that a lot of risk? Open risk for me, over that period of time, for a trade that's a high probability (maybe the highest) of making a lot of money? No.

7. Once the trade went onside, I'd taken that risk, so I would have to make $7,000 at a 1:1 risk reward. Is this justifiable risk? For a scalp, yes. For an average or a day trade? In this instance, yes. Open risk is mainly for scalps, but when you anticipate a big move and you have to get size in quickly, you have to be able to put the trade on no matter what even your own rules dictate.

This is the ultimate example of how pro and pro retail traders differ from that of retail. When I say 'right at the right time', this is it. You may only get one chance to get the size off and watch the trade go onside as it should do.

Yes, you can always get in later, but what if you don't? How many retail traders say 'if only I'd done this' and 'next time I'll do that'.

As a trader you tell yourself, when I get to do it again, I'll do it better, bigger. This is the difference in being a pro and pro retail trader. You get to tell the story because you went on to do it.

8. It wasn't a scalp, it was an event trade, an average trade. What is the acceptable reward? 1:2 $14,000, 1:5 $35,000. You don't know. You don't know how far the market will go. You know technical levels, you know what the average gold range is. What does it matter? I'm there to make money. That's what I'm trading for.
9. The market went in my favour, as I knew it would. Once the speed and size of the candles increased, I knew there was volume and interest coming into the market. The price went up quickly and the PnL followed.
10. The market consolidated for some short-term profit taking and then carried on in the trend direction. I took the profit for a PnL amount before it hit any of my major levels to avoid any sharp pull backs. At that point in time that was enough money from that trade for me.

That's how I made $77,000 in two hours with a 1:11 risk reward.

The only thing stopping you from doing this is the opportunity presenting itself and you knowing what to do with it. I've traded these types of events, so I knew what was possible.

I never thought about the profit in risk–reward terms. I never thought about how much I would lose. I had to balance the fear and greed emotions and focus on the entry, knowing if the entry was good, there was only ever going to be a massive amount of upside.

In all the trades I have a great degree of certainty in, I use size and take what I consider to be appropriate risk. This is how I make money as a pro retail trader. This is exactly what a pro trader does.

7. EMOTIONS WHEN TRADING

EMOTIONS OR FEELINGS are linked to different things for different people when it comes to life. It's sometimes easier to be motivated when you don't have much to lose and everything to gain. It can be harder to motivate yourself if you feel you have little to gain.

All I know is that everything is harder when money is involved. Unfortunately, as with any kind of business, which if done correctly, trading is, once you start getting accustomed to making money it is hard to stop.

Money is a good motivator. Controlling your emotions when trading your own money is a great leveller. When trading, making and losing money in the markets teaches you a lot about this.

My motivations and how I've dealt with my emotions have changed along my trading journey. Yours should too.

I wouldn't say it gets easier, but over time it becomes more manageable. Like trading itself, managing and harnessing emotions comes down to the experience gained from being in similar trade types time and time again.

This is why I broke my trading down into three trade types, two entries. All have different emotions attached to them. All of them combined have led to my overall goals over time.

Trading different accounts of different sizes also adds another emotional dimension and to some extent control. Trading accounts from scratch or with a drawdown have different emotions to those in profit.

No matter how experienced you are you will never fully be able to anticipate how each trade will make you feel in the moment. It's all about having as much control over your emotions as you can realistically expect from yourself.

It's about doing the right thing, the right trade type, at the right time.

Each time I trade it's a combination of the trade types, entry and account size. It's also about repetition. I've done every trade type many, many times before.

Emotions, feelings, however you want to phrase them, are down to you to control, manage or harness. While some traders or investors think you can leave emotions out of trading, I and other pro traders have found ways to deal with and harness their emotions. We use them.

My emotions explained:

> Controlled rage = is being hyper-focused.
>
> Fear = is not to be confused with being frightened. It's urgency.

Greed = is not to be confused with wanting more, it's wanting to get out what I have made. Protecting what I have (capital).

Doubt = is simply not sticking with the convictions of what I set out to do from trade types, entry type and account balance limitations.

Most of my emotions regarding trading mirror a sense of time. The less I think, the more I simply trade, the better I do. Trading just becomes a physical action. I know what I need to do. After all these years, everything that has made up my trading journey, my scalping style, is not much different from my first week on the floor. I just added more entries and then two more trade types.

WHAT I'VE PICKED UP FROM OTHER TRADERS REGARDING EMOTIONS

I've been around enough traders to see the full array of emotions. I've seen traders spit at their screens, smash their screens, stand up screaming and shouting, to being so broken by their emotions you see them sleeping under their desk. On the floor, off the floor, I've dealt with it all.

This was mainly from ex live floor traders. They were a product of that environment when aggression and bravado meant everything. Trading on the screens those emotions were not only wasted but largely counterproductive.

For the new breed of traders this wasn't the case. On the electronic floors the traders making, or even losing, the real money were deathly silent. It's not to say they didn't have emotions, of course they did, they just internalised them.

You can take the emotion out of a trade to some extent with a stop loss order. I choose not to do that. This is fine when you are trading well. The inevitable loss means very little. When you're not trading well for periods of time this can be more problematic. This is where pro traders have an edge by having a risk department. You will likely be stopped out before it ever gets too bad.

If trading success was as easy as simply trading with a stop loss then we'd all be millionaires. To make money trading, your emotions, risk and goals have to be personally adapted to each trader. There is no one size fits all.

When you meet successful traders, indeed successful people, which I have, at levels you'll never know, the first thing you realise is that they are just people. There is however something about them. It's that unique quality that sets them apart from the rest. I put it down to belief. Not in a spiritual way, but self-belief, people who can trust themselves in the decisions they take no matter what.

It's the perfect combination of self-assurance, wisdom, a gut feeling they can run with. It's people who have a high EQ, a reasonable IQ. Really intelligent people can be very hard work.

I can't really put it into words. When you meet these people, you just know, whatever *it* is they have *it*. I'm not arrogant enough to say I have *it*, but if you met me, maybe you'd say otherwise. This is the same with traders.

Everything from time, drive, to concentration, runs out eventually. Emotionally there is only so much of anything anyone can take. A little bit left field, if you compare trading to interrogation, so they say, everybody breaks eventually.

Most people and successful traders especially have come to terms with who they are. The ones who can recognise the emotions that bring out the best in them, harness them. Do well. They don't simply ignore them or pretend they don't have them.

SCALP EMOTIONS

I like the scalp trade the most as for me this evokes the emotions I can control and harness the best. The controlled rage, the fear, the greed. You may see these as negative emotions or weak feelings. I don't. I understand myself. I can't stress that enough.

The whole psychology aspect of trading, like technical analysis and fundamental analysis is both underrated and overrated depending on where you are in your own trading journey.

You can prepare mentally as much as you want.

> "Everyone has a plan until they get punched in the mouth."
>
> ***–Mike Tyson***

Why do rounds in boxing only last three minutes? Remember, I have a maximum of 15 minutes in a scalp. I'm not saying that going five rounds in the ring with Tyson is the equivalent of 15 minutes in a trade, but as an emotional metaphor, it works for me.

I can scalp this way during certain periods of the day. The conditions of the markets have to be exactly right for how I scalp. There has to be volatility, big moves and volume. Either way, if I don't take the pain, take the profit the first time it is offered, even I will eventually lose focus and turn a scalp into an average trade at some point.

It's important to recognise all the different emotions at this point. This is why monetary goals are important. I should be able to simply stop trading when I reach a certain amount of total profit. I shouldn't get to the point where I am emotionally drained and therefore make mistakes.

The key to trading and making money from a scalp entry when trading is to think less. The markets are going to do whatever they are going to do with or without you. No one is watching you trade; you are as individuals completely insignificant.

This is why I like scalping. When I am scalping well, it's almost like being on auto pilot. Some may also call this *trading in the zone*.

The controlled rage is just harnessing my emotions, it's tapping into and harnessing the fear and greed. Especially when trading as a pro retail trader or a retail broker I know my execution speed edge is less than that of the pros. I know I have to be lightning quick to almost pre-empt my entry and exit. This is the main reason I scale into trades to gain my own slight edge.

I've never filmed myself trading. I've sat with other traders for long enough to know that face though. There is a level of concentration to scalp, especially size. When you see it, or do it, as I have, it is truly one of the most satisfying ways to make money.

As I'm only in the market for small amounts of time, this is very important to observe. With scalping, the entry and exit are both equally important. You will only ever get one opportunity to get out at the max first-time profit offered. It literally may be available to you for a second. Emotionally this is where the greed will kick in. It's not exactly greed, more a sense of urgency.

Once I have put the trade on I only ever hold my mouse over my *close all* button. I know what downside amount I can take, I know how to watch the PnL and sense when the profit is right to be taken.

The experts say 'never look at your PnL'. That may work for investing or longer-term trading, but it doesn't work for scalping! Especially not pro retail trading.

The fear and greed are just a necessity of the trade itself, especially when using a fade entry. You have to be averaging into the extremes, especially when you are trading at market very quickly. You need to be in early enough to get a good spread of prices and to try to catch the market with your increased size before the market turns. The greed is much more about getting the size in rather than what you will make. The greed is making sure your entry and overall coverage is enough to make money from the pull back.

I have explained about *taking your money off the table* and *taking profit the first time it is offered*. This is the rule of a scalp. If you let true greed creep into your exit, and you change what you expect to make from a scalp, this rarely ends well.

I can't teach the controlled rage, but anyone can learn rules. Anyone can make rules. Not many people can stick to rules, even their own rules when it comes to making, and more importantly losing, money.

I have reached the level where I can bend and break my rules, but I really don't do it very often. There is a fine line between a rule-based trader and one who can adapt to the moment. Like being a parent; I think that's why there is no one book that perfectly explains parenting. The basics are pretty straightforward, anyone can take care of a child for a while. Being a good or even great parent over their life? That's a whole other thing. As it is with trading.

When I mentor people, they have to do the *baptism of fire*. Especially scalping. You have to put size into a trade that you have not done before. It doesn't have to be much more size than you have done before, but it does have to be enough to focus your attention. All of your attention. It is only by doing this that you learn what you are emotionally capable of dealing with. Trust me. It's probably cheaper to at least try this, than having a loss you previously had by not trying.

Simply put, my emotions for a scalp are factored into the trade. In this way you don't actually have to deal too much with the emotional side. If the emotional side does start to affect me, it's a key trigger to me that I'm doing something wrong. I've at times done hundreds of scalps in a single day. How many have I done over my career as a trader? I have no idea. It's a fight or flight situation. You get the size in and the average right you win or you lose. Maybe this is why I prefer it. It's not for everyone, I understand. The repetition and trading muscle memory is just ingrained in me.

This style is easier for the pro trader, I will explain this as DMA vs retail. Unfortunately, the reality is when you trade as a pro retail trader with a retail broker, the pure functionality means you have to take more pain and risk than those with DMA.

Once you understand yourself, and I do mean truly accept who you are as a person, you can't even entertain trading size scalps. How you deal with situations and your feelings and emotions is personal to you. Trading, more accurately trading real money, making real money, will test you like you have never been tested before.

AVERAGE TRADE EMOTIONS

The emotions and feelings that I have when trading anything other than a scalp include some form of anxiety. Time has always been the enemy in trading for me. My personality and my makeup as a trader are that I want to make and bank money as quickly as I can.

Is anxiety the best word? Maybe not. Doubt? I don't get stressed or fear losing money. It's more the money I've made when not being there anymore that comes into play when adding more time to a trade type. Where there is greed, there is urgency in scalping. When averaging I would say 90% of the time an average trade will go on side. Maybe not by much, but if the average is well placed, the market more often than not will initially go my way.

This is the main difference between the scalp and the average trade. I'm waiting for a bigger move over a longer period of time. I know I must leave money on the table. More time means more reasons to let the doubt creep in. To combat this is just conditioning. Most of what I do is just repetition. Although each trade in its own way is different, I'm sure for all the trades I've placed, I will have done the exact same trade at some point.

Dealing with the doubt involves a bit of self-talk. I talk to myself quite a lot during trading, in my head of course. I am never looking to justify a trade. I'm always asking questions based on what I know to be true. The biggest mistake I've made in the past is believing that the market *has to do this*. It doesn't and when you add more time to a trade the more opportunity the market has to prove you wrong.

The questions will vary as to what trade entry type I'm using. When using a follow entry I will ask more questions on what will happen (the future to the right of the charts).

When using a fade entry I focus more on questions about what has already happened.

Examples:

1. Has the market retraced to a key Fibonacci level?
2. Has the market come close to my trade stop amount?
3. Have correlated markets moved in a way I expected?
4. Have I been in this situation before?
5. Are my size, average and therefore entry moving in a way I have seen before?

In a way it's more giving myself the permission to stay in the trade. It's not all about what the charts and markets are telling me; it's also being self-aware enough to know how I am dealing with a trade. I know from bitter experience if I talk myself out of holding a trade and get out, the market will do and does exactly what I was expecting. We have all been there.

Having a monetary stop rather than a physical stop provides the discipline to allow a trade to breathe. I find the markets are so efficient now that holding a trade for anything longer than a scalp risks being prematurely stopped out. This is why I don't trade with the standard 1–2% risk of capital on each position. It's simply impossible to do when you average into trades.

Managing the emotions comes with the control of being able to hit the *close all* button as quickly as I can for a win as well as a loss. Losing in trading is simply part of trading. I don't take as many average trades as I do scalps. So there has to be a fixed monetary stop in my head. Once this is in then the real focus comes in managing the greed. The time element still has to play an important factor.

I've had the big wins, but I know that there is only so much you can ever expect to get out of each trade type, unless something unexpected has happened to change the immediate market sentiment. It's all about going back to the pro, retail pro and retail trader mindset. A pro trader will know. I know, as a pro retail trader what a good monetary win is. I know how much these types of trade from the eight markets I trade, the size I'm using, can potentially make.

This is the point you must get to. You need to know by pure repetition what amounts, in what markets, over what periods of time, you can make.

DAY TRADE EMOTIONS

Day trades have brought me some of my biggest monetary wins. They mostly are not always my biggest sized trades. With the added time spent in the trade you will get the positive of having more pip movement. The negative side, if you are me, are all the emotions that come with it.

I use different accounts to do different trade types at the same time. There is only so much logic when day trading of spending your time monitoring the PnL and sitting in front of your screens. There is the opportunity cost, leaving money on the table. Emotionally banking a good win over a great win still gives you positive momentum.

This comes down to experience, where you are in your trading career. It comes down to your motivation. I have said without my big day trade wins, maybe, I would not be where I am now. It's all about balancing out your trading journey. Big wins don't happen as often as small wins. The momentum those bigger wins give you, however, is invaluable.

I make no apologies for saying this again. All pro traders I know have at least one big win story. They were all a combination of size and time. Less than one day.

Day trades begin to slip away from my core principles of trading to make money quickly. People may think making close to six figures in eight hours is good. I can't argue with that, but when you can make four or five figures in minutes and hours, it's all relative.

I want to make money, I'd love to do more big day trades. The reality is that picking a top or a bottom of a market is not, in my experience, the best way to make money in trading. It's short-term investing. Retail traders are sometimes obsessed with tops and bottoms and where the market will go. There are so many pips to be had in the meantime in the range. This is because they do not make each pip count. They need a lot of movement to make any kind of money.

When dealing with a day trade, emotionally it will be a follow entry. My clip size will be lower and all I focus on is building a position around an area of interest and getting the trade onside.

The emotions of a day trade are very similar to that of the average trade. The doubt factor is just directly associated with more time. To control the emotion of a day trade you could at this point, if you wanted to, put in a stop and simply leave the trade. I don't do this. I will always watch a trade for its entirety, as you just never know what will happen.

Even though I assign up to eight hours for a day trade it doesn't mean that this will be the max profit point. Markets will move, consolidate, continue in the trend direction then will always eventually bounce. To what extent depends on the reason for the move.

Once the consolidation period of the trade is over, and the market continues to move in the initial trend direction, this is where the emotions, to a lesser extent doubt, but more so fear, come back. I control these by setting a monetary target or just setting a close for each candle as a time target.

Either way, the easy part is taking the money. The hardest part, that most retail traders ever do, is using sufficient size to make a good trade a big money trade.

SUMMARY

Much of what I've learnt over my time trading is, at some point, you just have to give up. Give up believing you must know everything. From technical analysis, to risk, to even believing you are truly capable of distinguishing between news and narrative and how you are told the markets react and the reality of how they will react.

Once I let go of the idea that, if I just knew more, I would make more money trading, then those feelings of frustration and the emotions linked to ultimate control went into the background. They didn't go away, but I could better focus on the emotions I did have when trading, not simply my idea of *the way trading should be done*.

Controlling your emotions in the markets comes from understanding yourself. You are your worst enemy in the markets. Reduce the time you spend in trades. Only trade when the markets suit your rules, set ups, trade types, whatever you call it. Only you can find a way of emotionally dealing with and trading the way you can in order to make money.

Stop trying to be right all the time. Be right at the right time for you. Once you make every trade about the money, taking that money from the markets, you get momentum. Once you get momentum you can scale up. It can take no time, it can take a lifetime. It will depend on how open you are to stopping trying to be the trader the world tells you you should be. Instead, focus on being the trader you need to be to make money.

8. THE *PRO* PART OF PRO RETAIL TRADING

I'VE PICKED OUT three fairly recent trades that demonstrate pro retail trading. What is achievable with a relatively small account and ones that are better funded. I have turned a $30,000 account into a six-figure account in a few hours. Probably down to more of that *luck* stuff. To an extent these trades and profits in theory can be achieved by any trader. I mentor traders with five- even six-figure accounts all the time. This is all achievable. So why don't they make these kinds of returns?

This is how pro and pro retail traders trade. They wait for the opportunities that have a high probability of making money. This is why traders at this level spend their time in front of their screens, or always have the ability to trade at short notice. I'm never that far from my trading set-up or at worst can trade from my phone. As a pro retail trader, I don't need as much time in front of the screens as I did as a pro.

Some retail traders often invest a massive amount of screen time but rarely produce these kinds of results. Why? They don't have the pro element. They invest too much time in learning account trading rather than doing it and focusing on making money.

Retail traders are usually doing trades for the first time. Making any kind of real money for the first time for retail traders is almost like a *job done* moment. It's not. It's just the very start of real trading.

The thing that separates retail and pro and pro retail traders is that the latter can do it again and again. Bigger and better. I've traded similar trade types and set-ups multiple times. I've traded big events a number of times. This comes with simply staying in the game long enough. I know what to do and more importantly how to make money, also what amounts of money I have achieved.

The key difference is knowing how much money I've made before and whether I can make more than that. Which consistently I have.

Trading is and should be a profession to you. A pro has made their money from trading. Many retail traders have made their money from something else and simply see trading as another avenue to make money from. It can be, but ask yourself how long it took you to make the money you're using. Simply having capital does not instantly make you a trader.

Pro trading is the ability to use size when it counts. You don't make big amounts all the time. Many retail traders just think if you can get the consistency and make a $1,000 a day then that's how you make money trading. Basic maths, $1,000 a day, 200 trading days in a year, you make $200,000.

This is not how it ever works in reality.

Pro and pro retail traders know, I know because I've done it, that this is the minimum you should aim for in a day. There will be winning trades, there will be losing trades. Invariably you will at times have bigger losses than $1,000. The consistency that every pro retail trader strives for really translates into the ability to come back from losses. Consistently make losses back and therefore add to overall profits.

It may be that in a typical trading day you may actually have up to 50%, yes 50%, of your trades that break even or lose or lose more than your $1,000 a day target. So what are you left with? It's not $200,000 is it? Remember with a pro trader you also have fixed costs to factor in.

Pro and pro retail traders know that you do need to make a base amount every day, or every time you trade. This will have to be in the thousands. The bigger trades where you use bigger size, the trades that come every week, month and year are where you will make a big chunk of your overall profit.

As a pro retail trader, you don't use big size all the time. The size has to be reflected in the probability of the trade. This really is the pro part. The momentum that comes from a bigger win, the motivations, the physical ability to trade bigger size after adding money to your account from a bigger win, is how you make money trading.

PRO MONEY

The FTSE scalp I have shown here is probably in a nutshell the best way to illustrate my pro retail trader style vs the reality of how the pro traders make money.

Pro trader:

1. A pro can put 1,445 lots in one or two clips (seconds) at individual prices.
2. Pays no spread.
3. Can get out at market or put orders in to get out at specific prices (seconds).
4. Risk is managed by risk department and/or may even see no offside risk (seconds).

Me:

1. I have 17 entries (individual clicks) at market prices (moving) that take two minutes.
2. Pay a spread – adds to offside risk amount.
3. I exit all trades via *close all* button at market. Not guaranteed at the same price.
4. All the risk is mine and psychologically you will see higher offside amounts for longer – two minutes.

Unless you have pro trader DMA you can't physically execute the trade as quickly. It's not possible.

Retail rules will make it impossible to justify this kind of size and open risk. This is why so many retail traders fail. They think they have to trade according to someone else's rules.

Pro and people like me, pro retail traders, trade to their own rules and more often than not get the rewards.

PRO ENVIRONMENT

When anyone starts trading, it is much harder to trade for yourself outside of a professional environment or at least in an environment that lends itself to making money. Anyone that says they sit on the beach and trade is a moron. There is always something else to do or distract you. I have an office set up at home and ever since the early days I have been able to separate my work from my home life that suits my trading. This is part of the pro set-up and mindset.

When I finally built my house, I had a six-month stream of visitors. Even though I had my office and space, this in monetary terms wasn't a great trading period. Obviously, I can't blame other people, but it's important to remember that being a trader is a difficult thing. Traders, well every trader I've met, hate change and any new environment or outside distraction can affect the mindset you're in, any subtle or not so subtle changes to your environment have to be managed.

One of the benefits, which is also a drawback to some extent, is that I trade mostly at night due to my location. There are fewer distractions. I'm not as young as I used to be, so I can't simply operate 24 hours a day anymore. Being a family man in the day and a trader at night, I truly have to let the markets come to me. If I can't stay up to see the trade through I don't trade; I accept I may miss opportunities. Which I often do.

The Asian session is still at times volatile enough to trade. This means I have to arrange my trading around sessions where I think the market conditions will suit me. I'm generally looking for lots of volatility, so this is in the aftermath of big economic data, when markets are being directionally driven by sentiment or when there are just busy trading periods. A power nap in the day can help with this if I need to stay up.

A power nap on the trading floors was a common occurrence for a lot of professional traders.

This is very easy to plan out from a fundamental perspective. All the information is right there on the economic calendars. If it's *high impact* it can mean movement. It also doesn't mean you should trade it just for that reason or convince yourself you know what will happen.

Since the markets are still predominantly traded by people you still get quiet holiday periods. There are times when nothing much seems to happen. When you trade professionally there are periods of time where you just sit on your hands and do nothing.

This is one of the differences between retail traders and the pros. Retail traders want to trade, pro traders want to make money. Retail traders will almost always over-trade.

TRADE OUTSIDE THE BOX

When I started to trade as a pro retail trader, I had to really decide what I wanted the most. Of course, it was money, but the time was also a major factor. It's not that the time on the floor was wasted, I just thought it could be spent in better ways. Due to the size I use and my trading style I don't physically spend that much time in actual trades compared to how many trades I did on the floor.

When you decide this, you have to then expect there to be a literal trade off. You won't catch every move. I accepted this. It's factored into my overall monetary goals.

If you want all the money from trading and to be at the top pro level of income, you must dedicate your life to it. It becomes your life.

Once I accepted this new hybrid model of trading, I was a lot more content with both my trading and my direction in life.

Now, I'm not trying to sell this as some fairy tale *I've got the best of both worlds* scenario. No matter what type of trader you choose to be or how you choose to trade there will be obstacles. It comes back to time, money and opportunity. This is why when I'm trading well, I trade with bigger size.

I make money when it's the right time for me to do so. It also helps with momentum, which I will repeat as being one of the most underrated things in trading.

BIGGER SIZE

I trade size when I feel the outcome is almost certain. This is how the pros trade. Keeping your clip size high stops the boring trades from happening. This takes a lot of discipline. You can actually miss a lot of good trades. It can also be hard to start a trading session, as no trader wants to start with a loss.

There are ways I have found to deal with this:

1. I trade different accounts.

I can trade accounts that are in profit as you have more confidence and in a way money to play with. It's not a game, of course, but emotionally there is no better way I know of tricking or convincing myself that trading from a position of profit is the same as from a position of drawdown. The emotions are different.

It's good to start slightly smaller sometimes and build up to size. It can never be too small or what's the point in trading at all. I'm here to make money after all. Trading with instant profits is a great example of how to gain quick momentum in trading. However, in my book, a small win can mentally be as bad as a loss if you are just trading because you can. This is the enigma of trading. You have to get to a point where every pip counts and yes I could have always made more, but if it's a trade that's in the thousands not the hundreds it is still worth the risk. This is something I've always pushed myself to do. Set a minimum benchmark level of money which I trade for.

2. My screens are always on but I have alerts and use my phone to watch the markets.

It's very easy to set alerts and monitor the market movements from your phone. You can always trade from your phone, though I don't advocate it. I've done my fair share and it's a different experience. I've never really lost when phone trading, but then again going back to my points above, it was never with any real size, so what's the point.

Working as a pro retail trader at home you have to find ways to both enjoy your time and be able to trade at a moment's notice. You must know what to look for and the market conditions that suit you.

3. Set daily, weekly, monthly and yearly targets.

When you get to my level and can make big money quickly it's just a matter of time and being in front of the screens when it matters.

Setting daily targets (based on your monthly and yearly targets) gives you something to aim for. Most retail traders want to make money, but they don't have realistic or quantifiable goals. So how do you know if you are winning?

I set a yearly target which reflects what I'm doing for the year. If I know I am doing something big, like building a house, I may want more money. If nothing is planned,

I may need less money. It's always important to have a baseline of what you want to achieve. Call it a wage or profit that you want to physically take out. After all, what are you doing this for? Just to build up an account? If you never make the money real, the money you hold can start to lose meaning.

TRADING IN DRAWDOWN

It's not all sunshine and rainbows. I don't always trade well, win or make the big money. I, like every other trader, have losses and periods of drawdown. When I get it wrong on any trade type it can be costly.

Trading in a period of drawdown can be very hard even for the pros. No trader likes taking a loss, but ultimately it will be how well you take your losses that will define overall success for most traders.

I trade averages with no stop. This is a dual-edged sword. I never know exactly how much a loss will be. As I always close all trades in one go, I have to be pressing to get out as my monetary stop approaches. There is no guarantee when retail trading that you will get out exactly at that point in time.

I do have a monetary stop. However, on the other hand, I can get out of trades for a win, small win, breakeven or small loss most of the time. With a stop, other traders are simply stopped out for their fixed loss.

This is not for everyone. Again, if it was easy, everyone would do it. I trade within my own framework that is personal to me. I've lived my life by my own rules, I trade the same way. It's incredibly difficult to be a true individual both in the markets and in, dare I say it, real life. The buck stops with me. I'm responsible for every trade, good, bad or ugly.

It can be an incredibly lonely existence when you realise that only you are responsible for you. It is also liberating, if you can handle that.

So how do I deal with this? Simple. You just carry on. Like with life, when it's maybe not going your way, you just move forward every day. It doesn't have to be a lot, but you keep on moving. Print green wherever you can.

In trading terms this means going back to basics. Scalping. Cutting your averages down. Lowering the size of my trades. I make no apologies for repeating myself again! Momentum. Getting momentum back, making smaller wins, any wins, moves you forward and changes your mindset. I tell myself over and over again, one loss, a bad trade, a series of bad trades even, doesn't suddenly make you a bad trader.

Going back to what consistently works. Going back to the trade type where you have made the majority of your winning trades, not the biggest trades, is key to getting back to profitability trade by trade, day by day.

Never chase and try to make losses back in one trade.

Accept that my losses came from having a trade type that was not right at that point in time. Like most other traders, we can all spot the moves, but how many times does that trade do exactly what you expect it to do when you exit the trade? The next candle? The next day? You have to take each trade on its own merit. Depending how good you are at keeping up your momentum, this will play a large part of how you handle trading in drawdown.

It just mainly requires common sense and some perspective. Time. Carrying on, not giving up and staying in the game is the only way to have a long-term trading career.

When trading goes wrong, and it will, you need to see what you did wrong. For me it's almost always staying in a trade for too long. I've traded enough to know this. I've traded enough to know why I do this. This is mostly because I want the market to do something it's not ready to do at that time. I'm very rarely wrong on direction, but then so are most traders.

Every pro trader who has made big money that I have worked with or risk managed at some point has taken on too much risk. Every pro trader I know has had losses and bigger losses than they wanted to take.

There has to be an amount that is practical, meaning it won't affect your ability to trade, and is also emotionally reasonable enough for you to simply carry on and it not phase you.

The main difference is that losses break retail traders. A pro trader will be able to bounce back and carry on, the same with a pro retail trader.

The only way to get back a loss is to stop, regroup and carry on trading the same way, or stop regroup and cut your size down and trade the best way you feel most comfortable with to make winning trades. I wish, for my own benefit sometimes, I knew or had experienced another way of doing this. I have not.

9. DMA VS RETAIL

As I've explained, when trading on a retail platform you don't have direct market access, DMA. This is when you have your own mnemonic, you trade through your clearing house directly with the exchange. The obvious advantage is the ability to trade large size at speed.

I have done this, through different houses. As a pro retail trader, I trade on a retail trading platform. There is a huge difference.

You have to accept if you're not paying for all the bells and whistles of DMA then all you are left with is the retail broker you choose to use.

SIMULATED MARKETS

When talking about retail trading platforms and brokers, I need to make it clear that this is trading on simulated markets. A retail broker will have its own book of traders and will have multiple liquidity providers. You are not trading with the exchanges.

It's not that much of an issue. This is the world you choose when you trade as a retail or pro retail trader. You pay via the commission and or spread. Retail brokers are not a charity, they are a business.

They will usually have a dealing desk so large orders or traders with a lot of volume may be managed.

There are a few things I've learnt trading this way:

- When scalping I look at my PnL. Trading for such a short period of time, when you are trading the size I sometimes do, money that was there one second may not be there the next. This is because of the above. My PnL may slow down and glitch, freeze or jump because of the systems the retail brokers have in place. I know this and I am prepared for it.
- What I see in my PnL action is not the same action I would see in the real market. I accept this. I use this and I know to be constantly aware of it.
- When the educational experts say never look at your PnL, they are talking about running a trade and not being distracted by the monetary value. When you're a pro retail trader you have to look at the money all the time; that's literally where the money is, especially when scaling and averaging into trades.

BLAME THE BROKER

People love to blame the brokers when they lose money, but the reality is the money was usually there to be taken, people just don't take it quickly enough. Sure, there is slippage and sometimes bad fills. Most regulated brokers will want their traders to ultimately make money and keep trading volume.

There are brokers that may not be the most trustworthy out there, but again this is retail trading. This is just all part of the understanding of that kind of business. I've only traded with a couple of brokers, ones who have a vested interest in making sure I'm happy. On the whole I've been able to trade how I wanted and certainly never blamed any broker for the outcome of my trades.

If you are not happy, become a bigger move valuable trader or find a better retail platform or broker.

SPREAD COSTS

If you have to worry about spread costs you are doomed from the start as a trader.

Spead costs will vary from broker to broker and will increase or decrease on implied volatility risks. This is why I only trade eight products. They are all institutionally accepted, and the volumes are there. If you want to trade the *exotics*, then you have to pay for the associated risk. What's an exotic? That's what Google is for. Do some homework.

Spread costs have to be in some way factored into your trading style. You will get options from most brokers. They call them different things like prime accounts where you pay a small fee per trade and get a lower spread. This is the *cost* you pay for retail and pro retail trading.

Is it cheaper than pro trading? Yes. Is it worth it? For me, yes.

I do size, volume and average into my trades. I do this to compensate for everything that is different between DMA pro trading and trading with a retail broker.

CLIP SIZES

There are maximum clip size limits set for retail brokers. When you get big enough this can change. For most people each product has a max clip allocation of around 100 lots.

Be aware that when clipping max size there are systems in place to pick this up and maybe send it to the dealing desk. This can lead to delays. They may be miniscule but when you are looking for a time and speed edge this is something to consider.

If the max clip is 100 lots, I may do 80 or mix it up with 77 lots. Why? The reason is that it is not the max clip. I find I get filled on most of the sizes I do when mixing up the clip sizes. I still get filled on most orders, but from experience and from knowing how retail brokers work I know this is worth doing. Max lot clips can be flagged and put into a different part of the book.

If you trade any kind of size it is always good to speak to your broker. Discuss account types, liquidity pools you can access. I have my own private group chat with my broker.

TICKS AND LOTS

A *tick* in pro trader terms is a price movement. A *lot* is the minimum amount size you can clip on a product.

This is where retail markets differ. You still talk in lot sizes, but the retail market movement works in pips and points. It was a lot simpler in spread betting when it was quoted in monetary amounts: $1 per point.

There are only two reasons I would ever trade on a demo account: to check out the lot size of the products I trade and to see what those amounts equate to in movement.

A THIRD REASON

A third reason to trade on a demo account, which you can do in the pro environment by the way, is to test out averaging in clip sizes to total trade amounts. This way you can physically see what the amounts and PnL movements look like in real time.

Don't confuse a demo account with being real, however. Obviously, it's not. What's very important to realise is that the demo account will work the same as it does with your broker.

Follow me here. Trading retail you will be trading simulated live markets. So not with the exchanges. You will get filled via the broker's book and liquidity providers *not* via the exchanges.

With a demo account you will be filled by a computer simulation. So not only is it not with the exchange, it's not with the broker's book either. All fills will be instantaneous, all orders will be filled and all your exits will always be filled at what you see. It's not a market at all. Everything is infinite.

So whatever you do on a demo account is never exactly what you can do on a live retail trading account.

A demo account can be very deceiving in terms of real results for pro retail trading. You will also never be able to attach any emotional connection to trades, or learn anything about what you would really do in a live environment. That's just not possible. I know from experience.

LEVERAGE

After the ESMA regulation lots changed for the UK retail broker market, the ability to use leverage was cut down. Leverage is a tool. If you want to use leverage, then there are brokers that offer more than others. Most of the spread betting world has now been replaced with CFDs (contract for difference). I use a broker that offers the leverage I want to use. However, I rarely use the max of 1:500 but leverage is still out there.

LIMITS

As a pro trader on the floor your trade size limits will be assigned by the risk department. You can have significantly higher limits than what your account size will allow.

As a pro retail trader you can choose to use leverage. You have to fund your own limits, which is why you need to start with a reasonable size. I'd say $10,000 is the absolute minimum. Above $25,000 the odds of the size you can then use and make money from significantly increases. But that's it. It doesn't mean much else without everything I'm covering regarding pro retail trading.

MOVING THE MARKETS

Institutional traders trade very large market-moving size. They have their own way of accessing markets and spreading the impact they will have on the markets they trade.

Pro traders rarely trade that size, but with DMA they can trade a larger amount of size and be much more price specific than a retail trader.

I don't as a pro retail trader trade enough size to move the market. I can however change the broker's book. Remember as a retail trader you are not trading with the exchanges, you are trading simulated markets with liquidity providers.

This is just something else to think about when trading.

MARKET NEUTRAL BROKER

You may choose a market neutral broker or execution only broker. This means they have no *B book*. This is where the broker can trade against client positions. It's not as bad as it sounds; after all, you were going to trade your trade anyway.

Most brokers use multiple liquidity providers, so there will be an element of hedging at some point anyway.

It's a grey area ethically for me. I tend not to use very big brokers as you become a very small cog in a big wheel. You become just another account number. Even at my level I prefer a broker who has a vested interest in keeping me happy and using my volume to make their profits.

It's all a business. There should be enough money in trading for everyone to make money from it. I accept this and again it is simply part of pro retail and retail trading.

WHAT YOU CAN TRADE

Retail trading and CFDs are a great way to trade thousands of products. Having capital in your account allows you to trade anything from crypto to shares.

This is different from the professional world as you can only have limits in certain products. As you are trading with the exchanges you need permission to trade different products and therefore the exchanges they trade on.

Be careful what you wish for. I can trade, in theory, anything that moves. I don't. I'll come to the reasons for that later.

REPUTATION

There are a whole other host of things retail traders worry about and talk to me about. Safety of funds, who brokers are regulated by, etc. Do your homework. I trust, as much as anyone can trust anything with brokers, the ones I trade with. This is because they are owned by people I've met and know personally. You probably won't have that luxury.

10. MOTIVATION

MOTIVATION WHEN STARTING OUT

SINCE AN EARLY age I have talked about having money and making money. Money interested me. Obviously, I knew money meant you could buy things. More than that, I could appreciate that money gave you power, freedom, control, but most of all time to do what you wanted to do.

I was told once, "Think of life like three equal sized ropes: time, money and opportunity. The more you pull on one, the less you get of the others."

Now earning money is easy. Well, it was for me. I was motivated by money, so I just went out and got it. I never had any issues getting a job. When you are motivated by money but also by the idea of making money, the above has much more relevance.

This is why trading appealed so much to me. I never saw the point in working for someone else for them to make money off you.

When I came to start trading, this is how I approached it. I was willing to put in the time, I had the opportunity, I wanted the money. It all seemed simple. However, this *job* was not a job as there was no salary. I didn't fully appreciate this.

Looking back, I definitely fell into the retail trader category of 'I need to make money'. Why I think my chapter about retail traders is particularly important is that every trader is a retail trader until they *make it*.

Knowing very little about pro trading before this, I just assumed I'd made it by being there. I was automatically going to get rich quick. My plan and my motivation had to fit in with my expectations of myself. I liked the idea of getting rich quick, of course, but I also needed money to live on.

As I saw it, I had to tie the money and time rope together. Give it a good pull. Really use this opportunity.

I started trading bigger size not because it was an ego thing but because it was a necessity. It was encouraged and mainly because you were paying to be there!

My first experience of pro trading was a bit of a roller-coaster ride. Having had a big win early on, in my mind I'd done what I set out to do. To a very small extent I'd *got rich quick*. I obviously wasn't rich, but I'd made what I considered at that time to be big money.

I spent too much time trying to replicate that trade, which was the worst thing I could have done.

What's apparent to me now is that I was financially underprepared. I'd ended up working for myself, but really working for someone else, my backer Refco. This was a valuable learning curve for me.

My next experience of being a pro trader I was much better prepared for. I'd taken *jobs*, well-paid jobs. Jobs that would allow me to know much more about trading than simply learning more about trading. Jobs that would show me how other traders made money.

I still had the making money motivation. What I did is not that dissimilar to what retail traders do. Wanting to learn more about trading in order to get better at it. Instead of learning more about trading, while in the risk room I learnt about how traders make money. That's not the same thing.

My new motivation was seeing how and what kinds of money were really being made. Knowledge is power so they say. Also wanting to see if I could actually do it.

Being on the floor I've seen it all. People having a good day, then going out and buying stuff. From Rolexes to Ferraris. Most people think trading is addictive and it gives you a buzz. It doesn't, or it shouldn't if you are doing it correctly. It's the making the money that is addictive, especially when you are at that rare level where you can instantly withdraw it without affecting your ability to trade and spend it almost instantly.

I fell into the trap of building up my account. There is nothing wrong with that. It's logical and sensible. Being the person I am, I needed something physical to show from the time I'd invested in my trading journey. That's how I was motivated at that time.

I needed to make the money mean something. The money was just numbers on a screen. I did this by replacing the money targets with a thing, something I wanted. It was usually a Rolex. Depending on how I was trading, that was a day or a week. This may sound petty and shallow. It was a psychological technique used by some of the motivational experts hired to be on the floor. This worked for me. I make no apologies for accepting my early superficial needs.

I certainly didn't smash it on the floor. I never became Braveheart. As I've explained, even if you're the lowest level of pro trader, you're doing OK though.

I'm not a team player, well, not when it comes to money. I'm not built that way. I often wish I was, but what can you do? Being part of a team on the floor just stopped working for me. The floor environment in general was no longer productive to my trading. There were too many egos, mainly my own.

> "I told you that we could fly. 'Cause we all have wings, but some of us don't know why."
> *–Michael Hutchence*

Once I decided to literally *back myself* trading everything changed. For me personally coming off the floor at that time made a lot of sense. I'd got enough from the pro trading world in experience and to a lesser extent, the very thing I was there for, money. I had money now and I could make it on my own.

Having just come out of the pro trading world, I never had the negative mentality of risk. Risk was mine to take and to make money from. I had the freedom to do whatever I wanted. Keep everything I made. This was motivation. This is the position I'd always set out to be in, what my journey has made me realise. You don't know what you don't know.

I made money, of varying degrees, over the days, months and years, I took breaks, but I never stopped. I traded and made money for myself. The only difference is that I did this as a pro retail trader and traded with a retail broker.

By cutting out splits and costs, I could make what I did as a pro so was 'up' from the start. This meant I could take out my own money whenever I wanted.

Finally, I ended up having my own *Rolex moment*. Actually, it was a chronograph Tag Heuer and I still have it somewhere. I made a great trade in a day and just went out and bought a watch I'd seen in a shop window.

Later on there were some more actual Rolex moments. Quite a few. I might have had a problem, which looking back was unnecessary and somewhat frivolous. I understand myself now, and as basic as it seems, at that time I was still motivated by things.

It was part of my journey and having something physical to show for my efforts had a purpose in trading, to a point.

If it's always just numbers on a screen it can start to lose meaning. Well, it did for me.

I was now at a level I could handle, now was the time to take it to the next level of size and start making money.

That was my trading journey to that point. Realising my initial motivations for making money and buying things. I had become a pro retail trader.

What now?

MOTIVATION WITH A PLAN AND A PURPOSE

Once the money started to roll in and the consistency of being able to trade size came into play, the world started to look very different. This did not happen overnight, but compared with the time I'd essentially spent putting myself in a position to back myself, it was not very long at all.

I was now trading multiple accounts and had all sorts of interesting trading related spin-offs. Like writing books. I don't think it matters how ambitious or sure anyone is that they will eventually *make it*. When you do it's never exactly how you think it will feel.

It took me a relatively long time from when I placed my first trade, to being in the position to then place trades so that I could get rich quick. I felt no shame in spending the money I'd made. There was no guilt. I'd started trading when I was pretty young. My original motivations were somewhat boyish but had got me to this point. Now a man, my motivations and goals had to change.

It took meeting the woman who would become my wife to really help me shift that motivation from buying things, into a motivation for using my money to achieve other bigger things. I remember sitting in some roof-top spa in Croatia not long after we met and I told her, this is what I'm going to do, I going to make this much a month. What I thought we should then do with the money I made.

This was the next step in unlocking my motivational wants and needs, having trading goals and to some extent a higher purpose for what I was doing all this for. Motivation is second only to momentum in trading for being underestimated and misunderstood. You need to set big goals (personal to you) and achieve those goals, whatever they may be, to be able to move forward with any real meaning.

I'd been a lone wolf for a long time. It was time to become the leader of a pack.

This is the first time I'd actually made a significant plan, put some thought into what I wanted to make and more importantly what I wanted to do with the money I'd make. This again is why the retail trader chapter is so important in this book. It covers all stages of trader I have met.

I guess what the big picture goal was, what I wanted out of life. I had an idea of what my life should look like, now I had finally grown up, or, at that level of trader, made it.

I knew how to make things happen, but I needed to make them happen, as it turns out, unbeknown to me. I needed to do this for someone else rather than just myself.

As simple and straightforward as I was, the complexity of who I am meant I needed someone else in my life, to really feel alive and to motivate me to get to the next trading level. This was new to me. I hadn't expected this at all.

The details of the plan aren't that important, or even that interesting. It was simply money and time frame orientated. What's important is that I had one.

That plan is why I am where I am today.

Everything I said in that plan, I did. The goals I set I achieved. More importantly, what I wanted to result from those goals I now have. I'm writing this book, sat in my office in the house I built, on the expansive land I own, in the *arse end of nowhere* in New Zealand. I have the cars, more stuff than I ever wanted. I'm married, I have a daughter, two dogs, and yes, still have the watches. Though they live in the safe as I don't need or have much need or real desire to wear them.

Never be told what's the right motivation or reasons for doing what you want to do in life. Find them however and wherever you can. Whatever, and I do mean whatever, works for you.

11. I CAN TRADE ANYTHING THAT MOVES BUT I DON'T: WHY?

It is very tempting to simply trade the next big thing or whatever is moving right now. A lot of this is driven by the MSM, advertisers and people with something to gain. I'll say more on that in Chapter 13. Depending how deep you want to go down the rabbit hole, who knows who else? One thing is clear to me. The rich and powerful only get richer and more powerful and that's accelerating at an alarming rate. We will no doubt soon see the world's first trillionaire before we end something like world hunger.

The most common question I'm asked when people know I'm a trader is: 'What should I be buying?' Like I have some kind of crystal ball. People are easily preprogrammed into believing there is something new out there that could make them their fortune.

This is why I don't tell many people what I do. It's just not worth it. They always know someone who did this, made money doing that, lost money investing in this and that, it's just a boring conversation for me that I have had too many times to count.

This is another reason for this book. People asked me what I did, how I did it. Here it is.

People get sucked into trading markets because they move, without fully appreciating why they move. This is because of the attraction of big pip movements and volatility. Volatility is good but only with volume. If something moves and there is no volume, it's very hard to scalp or get out when you are wrong, especially if you have any kind of size on.

Pro traders will trade things the retail traders will not. This is because they have a lot of institutional-level money in them. Therefore, they can trade against that big size. There is liquidity and volume.

This is why I stick to the main markets I do. They not only correlate, not always exactly how you want, but there is enough liquidity and volume across the board in those products to be able to scalp, average and day trade. I have the ability to be right and wrong and benefit from market movements in any direction.

While a lot of retail traders are interested in individual shares, crypto, NFTs and all the other *trendy* things, I'm not saying people can't make money from them. The reality of all these things is that there will be lots of people who lose money and a small number who make the majority of money from them. How many Bitcoin billionaires are there? How many Bitcoin millionaires are there? How many people have lost money to make that happen?

Trading the exotics, less liquid FX pairs and various other products that retail brokers offer lend themselves to the *big win* idea. You will be very right or very wrong. How many times can you replicate that?

I trade eight products. I know them inside and out. There is always ample liquidity for my entry styles and there will be at least one opportunity in one of those markets a day to trade. Being a pro retail intraday trader makes sense to me. There will obviously be more opportunities when there is volatility.

My view is that you make your money from the markets. When you have made enough profit that fits in with your goals, you take that money out of the account and use it. If you then want to trade something else, invest it, buy a Rolex, that's up to you.

Trying to master one market is counterproductive for short-term trading. You simply won't get enough trades unless you are trading very big size or are uber self-disciplined. Trader's trade. Traders need to trade. Trying to trade every market or the next big thing is asking a lot of anyone. It's all a balance.

Don't get distracted by what other traders are doing. This is one major factor in my leaving the floor. Who cares what anyone else is doing? Why waste any time, effort or focus on something you can't control? Focus on what you can do at your level right now.

12. MARKET NEUTRAL: WHY I STRUGGLE

THE BEST WAY by far to intraday trade and especially scalp is to be market neutral. By this I don't mean a strategy or hedging positions. This means you have no particular bias on why the price is moving. You just buy or sell short-term value based on movement. This is how I first started scalping on the floor.

In a lot of ways when you first start trading it is a lot easier to trade when you don't know that much. It doesn't mean it's easier to make money, but trading small amounts of price movements, quickly, is not too daunting as a concept. Over time, the more you know, or think you know, the harder trading can become.

Most retail traders and to an extent most traders all fall into the trap of wanting to learn more and know more. I was taught to a very high level. I learnt a lot very quickly. While it's important to have a level of understanding of all the important elements of trading, you can go too far. I certainly have gone too far at times in my quest for knowledge.

Being great at fundamental analysis, being great at technical analysis, being great at trading theory, doesn't necessarily make you a great trader. Or more accurately doesn't mean you will make money from trading.

I struggle to stop bias from creeping into my trading from the fundamental side. I read news in a different way from most people. I read all news from multiple sources, even the ones that are considered to be *fake news*. I'll make my own mind up about things, thank you world. That's the person and therefore trader I am. I'll explain this in the next chapter.

Much of the bias comes from the overall big picture. I don't invest, that's not what I do. It's very important I don't fall into the trap of expecting the market to do something, just because something is presented to the market as relevant news at that exact point in time.

After enough time, you will have your favourite trade types and markets you prefer to trade. Mine has always been the Dax. There is a lot to focus on with trading both consciously and subconsciously. We all want to know as traders where a market is going. Stock traders especially are obsessed with what they should buy next. Again, that's because stocks always go up eventually, right?

Retail traders are seemingly obsessed with where a market will go. They will go up, they will all go down. They often forget there are many corrections, pull backs, profit taking happening multiple times in any one directional trend. Being market neutral is just a simple way of trading within the trend. Taking smaller amounts from bigger moves.

This is why I have the three trade types.

With a scalp there is only so much bias that can creep in. This will be determined by the entry type I chose. With average and day trades it's practically impossible not to have a sliver of bias in your trade idea. It's just a time thing. If a market is moving in one direction it must be for a reason. I don't necessarily have to know why or agree with it, but size will come when a market moves in a direction I like.

I'd say I'm pretty good at being market neutral when scalping, though I still do have markets that I like to short more than others, which are gold and the EUR. If you can be market neutral this can help a lot with the emotional side of trading. The *trying to be right*, trying to justify why a market is moving.

I can't be and don't expect to be perfect at everything when trading. This is just something that is worth mentioning. It's mainly for you, not me. I've put this short section in just to remind myself that no trader can truly master everything even if they know it is important.

I've accepted this limitation in my trading and I know it's something I've still got to work on.

13. MY OLD 80/20 RULE AND MSM NEWS

ONE THING THAT has dramatically changed since my last book is my take on how information is presented to us. My 80/20 rule in trading was simple in principle: markets move 80% of the time due to technical information and 20% of the time due to fundamental information.

That is no longer the case. I see it much closer to 50/50: 50% technical and 50% news, information and now narrative.

What's increasingly clear, to me anyway, is that there is a huge amount of narrative flowing though the MSM news organisations and to a lesser degree the financial news. Well, a lesser degree if you're not trained on reading financial news, data and information, which most people are not.

I increasingly feel a large part of the population is suffering from an almost global news Stockholm syndrome. A lot of this has likely been triggered by global events such as the pandemic. People seem to dislike the news, some mistrust the news, but we are becoming increasingly reliant on it, maybe addicted to it.

I do not read the news like you do. I do not read financial-related news like you do.

As a pro trader I paid for the fastest access to news (mainly financial) and data that was available. A Bloomberg terminal, news feeds, a squawk. This was when the fastest finger first, with DMA, was a significant advantage in trading. I don't use these anymore. I'm much more prepared to follow the set narrative and see how the markets and other traders react in the markets, then trade accordingly.

I can't go into who I know, how I know things I know, to any real degree. It's just not worth it. I stay close to the money, the real money, but at the same time I am geographically as far away from it as humanly possible. Make of that what you will.

You lose all credibility when you talk about things people don't have the mental capacity to comprehend, which unfortunately translates to about 80% of the global population.

MSM NEWS

If you start with the MSM, it's increasingly owned by a small group of powerful individuals, which to a large extent it always was, but now it feels different. It's becoming much more one global coordinated voice. I myself have lived through the start of the idea of a *single source of truth* from a prime minister right here in New Zealand.

Take a global topic. I'll leave out the obvious one. Let's take climate change. Specifically *manmade* climate change. We seemingly don't have seasons or just weather anymore. We have a series of *weather events* and terms like *global boiling*, a *climate emergency*: a panic and fear-inducing narrative.

The MSM now tell us regularly that this is the hottest day, week, month, year or since a specific date further back in the past. More and more I also seem to read these changes are the most extreme 'since records began'.

When there is the potential for 5 inches of snow in winter, it's a *weather bomb* and a *red weather warning*. Almost like a coordinated cry of 'We're all going to die', which we are. That's the only certainty in life. It used to be death and taxes, but let's face it, that's contentious.

I've lived through greenhouse gases, which at one point we needed more of due to a global freeze coming. I remember watching that as a kid on *Tomorrow's World* on TV. Then it was acid rain, the ozone layer, global warming, climate change due to rising sea levels, etc. This is from my own memory, so it may not be in that exact order. You get the idea.

This is just a very small example of how a narrative is set by the MSM (and those who are behind them) and how easily people are drawn into believing the people who tell you the news, that they are delivering it for your benefit and not for another agenda. Funnily enough, the agenda on climate change (or whatever the current crisis or emergency is by the time you read this book) mainly revolves around whether it can be fixed, with more controls, regulation and *new* technology like wind farms and solar. It just needs more money, a lot more money and therefore more tax.

In Canada, as I write this, aggressive carbon taxes have now been imposed on individuals. Again, *imposed*, as no one voted for them.

It's not like I'm trying to predict the future, but if I were I'd say by 2030, which again is a date widely used in the media for a number of accords, agreements and agendas, a lot of personal freedoms we take for granted now like driving cars, air travel and the food we eat will be restricted due to its implied impact on the environment. By 2050 we will probably have been implanted with a digital ID with a carbon credit score, which would be enforced by the use of a central bank digital currency (CBDC).

You can believe in manmade climate change. That's your choice. You can believe me or not with regards to tax, money, power and control as the aim. That's your choice too. For the purpose of this book I'm not trying to say I believe it or not. It's simply about acknowledging whether there is a widespread, multi-layered, controlled narrative existing in the news.

The MSM at a very high level also sets the tone for what non-traders can expect from government policy, the central banks, things like interest rates, inflation and GDP growth.

How many times have you spoken to someone, and they have said: 'Well it's because of the economy'?

My job as a trader is to follow the money. I can't control the news, narrative or the markets. All I can do is control what I do with the information I have and how I choose to take it in.

BIG PLAYERS MADE THE NEWS

It's very difficult to predict what one trader with enough size can do, as we have seen with people like George Soros in 1992, who *broke the BOE* and crashed the GBP. Trades like that may be less possible these days. The markets are bigger, and maybe they are more prepared?

Central banks can still cause a shock with a policy decision, like Swiss National Bank back in 2015. In a surprise move, they removed the cap on the Swiss franc causing a *flash crash*. We may see at some point an FX intervention by the BOJ with the USD/JPY if the dollar carries on its bullish trend.

My point is that the ability to trade at a level to create news-making events is limited to only a select few. The MSM is the place where people hear about these things. Non-traders that is.

These news-making events are examples of what happened in the old markets. I personally think that the MSM, institutions, big players and central banks are much more coordinated now.

WHAT ABOUT FINANCIAL NEWS?

I believe big players now use news and narrative to collectively make money. It's not to say big news trades won't happen again, I'm sure they will. I think the MSM sets a tone. The financial news and government data that traders use are not less useful, but traders need to give them much more consideration now. I see the markets move on news much more than I have done in the past.

Are big players the news?

I still read news. All news. News will always be a part of trading. In my last book I referred to news sources such as the FT, Bloomberg, Reuters and all the other big names you'd expect. I've also been quoted in all of them. I read these news sources now and I don't see news, I see narrative. Not in all news, but it's there hiding in plain sight. I was always brutally honest when contributing to news. I say what I think. I don't care if it's what people want to hear or not.

Financial news doesn't work in trading the same way it did back then.

With social media and how people access information and news, it's easier for entities to personalise and target how likely someone is to read certain information. Twitter or now X *for you* is a good example.

One of the richest men in the world gets to show you news and information you're likely to read. All I know for a certainty about rich people is, they know other rich people.

My thinking, and again I'm happy to be proved wrong, is that collectively big players across the institutions, MSM, financial news and to some extent the central banks, are working more closely together. I don't see another way to explain the changes I have seen in the way markets now move.

If the same small group of people make money and the only downside is the unfortunate ones on the other side of the trades, and of course the taxpayer, is this that far-fetched?

The fact is we have more and more global billionaires. Elon Musk is a great example of this, when he said he could take Tesla (coincidentally posted on X) private at $420 a share. Not only was he made to step down as chair, but he and Tesla were fined $40m. Who made money, who lost money?

Now it's important not to get too drawn into this. I'm simply stating things I think about for you to at least question.

ME AND THE NEWS

I myself have been caught on the wrong side of what I know news and data should do to a market a couple of times. I'm hardly new to the game. I take pain, I do all the right things and have paid the trading price. I don't blame anyone but myself. Economic cycles change, how markets react changes. The only true constant in trading the markets is that they change.

I'm not simply trying to blame losing trades on some secret society that rules the world!

With most things I do, I take a look at myself first. Why do I feel the need to understand everything? Why do I need to be proved right when interpreting news or data? Simple: I don't. It doesn't mean I want to pass up good trading opportunities. This is where it can become very difficult as a trader.

When you look at growth numbers, NFP, GDP and inflation numbers like CPI, especially from the USA, then things don't stack up. I'll go over the data shortly. What the news and narrative say is happening in the economy is not what is happening in the day-to-day lives of the average person. I accept this to a degree, but when news is used to move and manipulate the markets, that's when, as a trader, it's much more important for me to understand.

During Covid-19 the central banks spent trillions on trying to avoid a recession. Now the money has been spent, interest rates have gone up to try to control the inflation this spending caused, while trying also to avoid a recession.

If I was being quoted, I'd write something like that to describe economically where we are currently.

Firstly, the stock market is not the economy. We hardly ever mention the word *recession* with regards to the economy anymore. It is now referred to as a *soft landing* or trying to avoid a *hard landing*. Why? Narrative. It's a better framing for something that is bad or very bad for the average person, but hopefully, in this case, not for the stock markets.

I see where we are economically as the same as the time, money and opportunity ropes.

You can't have high interest rates, high inflation and debt-driven growth. Something has to give eventually. The US interest debt payments can't come down without lower interest rates, both of which are unsustainable.

It may take time, a long time, but every bubble bursts. Inflation may come down to the 2–3% levels that are *targeted* by central banks, but without a level of prolonged deflation, there is still a huge amount of inflation already baked in. Prices may go up more slowly, but they have jumped dramatically in price until that point. Things don't just go back to the price they were without other factors.

War-driven GDP growth and manufacturing paid for by government debt can't last forever.

Bringing in other news narrative such as AI, what gives? Employment, jobs. Everyone can have more time and an easier life with AI. The way I see it is AI will just be another private sector excuse, as a traditional recession would normally be, to cut jobs. This time not manual or blue-collar jobs but white-collar jobs. What happens if we suddenly don't need accountants or lawyers?

We can't blame the central banks or governments, it's down to progress and technology.

Coming into what may turn out to be the most publicised US election ever, it's both a political narrative and I believe a way to benefit the people who will make money from it, in other words the biggest players (trading institutions) in the markets. If you look into it, which I have, these are essentially the same entities.

The economic commentary and narrative behind much of what I read is all designed for the top level of traders to make money from it. It's one big club and you are not in it. I know the club exists, I can neither confirm nor deny I know people in it. I am not in it.

Follow the money. Who gains the most from any news narrative?

This is why I day trade and I am not an investor. You can literally buy the narrative and make money all the way up. Until at some point you lose. Maybe it all. Maybe even more than that.

BIG PLAYERS, NEW NARRATIVE

So if the big players own the media, big players own the institutions and corporations. How much influence do they have on government? What happens if you have a big player who is a prime minister or president? We do, we did, and we may do again in November 2024.

I'm going to share my thinking with three examples of how I see narrative, big players, retail traders and taxpayers have been working in the markets more recently.

HODL NARRATIVE

Bitcoin. Who or what is Satoshi Nakamoto? The English translation from the Japanese 中本 means *central origin* or *(one who lives) in the middle.* Is it that far-fetched to think this was created by a government agency? CIA, NSA? I don't know. If it's so important to the future of civilisation, depending who you listen to, then why don't we know?

All I know personally is I'd want to know the very basics, like who invented Bitcoin before I traded it with any conviction.

There has been a HODL (hold on for dear life) narrative for some time with Bitcoin. It's a narrative within itself. Even if the price goes down, don't sell, buy more.

It's become almost a cult. The volatility and speed of the swings in the Bitcoin price are staggering. Even to someone like me.

I can understand the idea of buying a Bitcoin. I can't understand using a retail trading account to build a position in Bitcoin. It's decentralised. I get it. I'm not here to argue against Bitcoin. I'm just saying who ultimately wins? Who makes the most money from Bitcoin's movements? How many narrative events that would either make or break Bitcoin happened that never materialised?

All I know is that it's seen as the only alternative: you are either right or wrong. Very right, or very, very wrong.

There aren't that many big wallets. It's around 1% of wallets that hold over 80–90% of the total Bitcoin supply. The very definition of big players.

With the amount of volatility these few wallets can inflict on the market, there is no manner of stop or momentary stop that can be reasonably used. It's just a literal licence to whipsaw a market and take out the least prepared traders, which is usually retail traders, or if they HODL they can only be investors as they *hold* positions in one direction over time.

Now, I'm not saying people shouldn't trade Bitcoin. In fact now more than ever with so much institutional money, it's more suited to my trading style than it ever has been. I still see it as an investment or commodity over an actual currency. It's something I'd have to seriously think about before I was to day trade it.

STOCKS AND MEME NARRATIVE

When did senators become some of the best investors on Wall Street? Nancy Pelosi seems to be one of those that stand out. Her trades on Nvidia were pretty notable. There is plenty of information out there, places where you can even automatically follow their portfolios. If you can't beat them, join them I guess! Names like Brian Higgins, Mark Green and Garret Graves to name a few. There are probably 30 members of Congress that are beating the average hedge fund YTD right now, by a significant margin.

Now that's not necessarily a narrative, it's just people who have very privileged insight into legislation that could affect a stock price. It may just make the link between the big players and the government a bit more of an inconvenient truth.

> "If you don't know enough about economics, you will never fully appreciate politics. If you don't think economic policy is political, you're delusional."
> ***–Steve Ruffley***

This doesn't mean it's not useful to follow from a day trading perspective. Anything that moves can make a day trader money.

Stocks like GameStop (GME) and AMC Entertainment holdings (AMC) were probably not traded by senators; they were heavily traded by retail traders and institutions.

This narrative was, from my personal opinion, the most obvious one to end badly for the average retail traders. There seemed to be a David vs Goliath narrative where, because of information on Reddit and these *sub groups*, the masses could take on the *big guys*, the hedge funds and institutions and win.

From everything I know and everything in this book it should be clear that every retail trader, pro retail trader and pro trader needs to know their place in the markets. You don't become a better retail trader by joining up with other retail traders. You just become a collectively bigger target.

There is a real danger with the hysteria and FOMO created by narrative. Who can you trust? Who has the deepest pockets, most resources, who's been killing the competition the longest? It's the guys at the top. Those who have been doing this the longest.

The idea that with enough volume the collective could squeeze hedge funds and institutions out of positions is something you get away with maybe once. It's a one and done opportunity. Once traders buy into the narrative that they are winning, they have already lost. For every retail trader who made millions, there are plenty more that lost the lot.

The big guys may or may not have fuelled the narrative. Overall, they will have profited from this. That's just how it works.

There is a general powerful narrative that stocks can only go up. 'What do I buy next?' There is seemingly unlimited upside. Stocks are a risky investment. Just because the *dip* gets bought doesn't mean it will stay that way forever. The longer any trend continues, the harder it eventually breaks. I would say even by the time this book is published the global stock markets may look very different from where they are trading today.

When the next stock market crash comes, which it will, the vast majority of which is held by one generation, that generation will have very little time to make it back. The big players will make money on the way down and vast fortunes over time as it goes back up.

This will destroy the wealth for not only that generation but for all generations to come. If you're a big player, that's a win-win.

This is the difference between trading and investing. Even short-term investing. The key is to use the volatility, however it is created, to get in and get out intraday.

I don't know of a better way to explain the way I see narrative working in the financial markets and the fact that it continues to favour the upper echelons of trader types.

On another side is also what I see as *cult brands* that have a similar stock price mentality. This would be companies like Tesla, which feeds off the climate change narrative to some extent, which I used as an example earlier. This is an emotional attachment to a brand and a company to its leader. I think in the years to come this may well leave people both financially and emotionally disappointed.

DATA

You have to trust the data right? There was understanding on the floor that most data from China was to be taken with a pinch of salt. The data was always in line with expectations and was always too good to be true. That was OK, the market accepted it, and we just carried on like everything was fine. Who was it hurting though?

The data we are getting today right now from countries like the USA has come to be like that in my view. When Trump was president and started to comment on the non-farm payroll numbers, which most presidents left to the Fed, I could really start seeing the narrative and how trading data moves were really beginning to change in favour of the institutional traders.

This most definitely would have been for political reasons, but people listen to the president. Traders listen to the Fed and the BLS who compile the number. This moved the markets. Like a lot of things, Trump, the lines between power and influence and the money markets became even more blurred.

Follow the money. Who benefited most?

I have traded the non-farm payroll a lot in the past on the first Friday of every month. I very rarely trade it now. Even with my narrative adjustment and actually understanding the figures, it's become a bit of a lottery. The reality of the number that is presented, when you break the data down, is just a headline grabber with lots of holes and questions for a trader.

We seem to be replacing permanent jobs with part-time jobs, adding jobs that are essentially public sector. There are supposedly more jobs, but if the same people are having to take them, if a person now has three jobs, is that really a new-job-created scenario?

There has also been massive immigration into the USA. I can't go too far down the rabbit hole on that. Not in this book. Let's just say there are a number of ways to make the data do what you want it to.

With GDP figures, when you are running a $34tn debt (and counting – by the time you read this who knows), are you creating real growth? When your debt interest payments are more than the entire defence budget? Does that mean you are safer? Is the economy?

Inflation figures. Food prices are high, well that's inflation for you. Why are these companies making record profits? Is it because there is little or no competition? The data, the narrative, is manipulated and presented to people to make them think things are bad. They will get better: 'We have a plan.' At what point do you have to accept that this was the plan all along?

I don't want to spin off into a broader economic or societal tangent. I just follow the money. It's all going one way, out of the average taxpayer's pocket and into the ones at the top who own almost everything.

The main problem with data is I don't necessarily trust it anymore. Even if I do trust the data, there are many ways it can be easily revised down or recalculated and used to fit into the current narrative that is being set. Seasonally adjusted, ex auto, energy, the list goes on. New ways of calculating data that seem to constantly change.

Nothing is as simple as buying or selling good or bad data anymore. I have seen this as a trader since the 2010s. What does this 50/50 movement mean for trading?

For trading purposes data is still market moving, there are still opportunities to make money. It's not fastest finger first, like it was on the floor for me. It's not who best understands the economics any more. It's not even to go counter trend and trade against the narrative any more.

It's simply knowing your place as a trader in the current trading environment. It's knowing whether you have any edge or not by trading based on what you are told and what you expect you should then do.

Most of the financial narrative that is filtered through the markets comes from the central banks themselves. This has a term: *forward guidance*. This is where the head and the members of the Fed, ECB and BOE deliver information to the markets.

This will be hints and language used to tell the markets what may or not be happening prior to decisions on things like interest rates. Interpreting this requires an understanding. It's a skill. There will be key words that change and certain language to look out for to signal what may happen next.

This can be an opportunity for short-term traders to get on quick moves if the narrative or current sentiment changes from what has been previously said. The markets can be very volatile around these periods and much of the movement I see just goes to highlight that most of the moves that now happen are for the bigger levels of traders. The institutions and the central banks themselves.

I prefer now to trade much later from these events and trade the *aftermath*. I know my place as a pro retail trader and just try to scalp or at best average some of the moves. The pip movements can be extreme. If there is sufficient liquidity it can be a quick in and out and an opportunity to trade the movement itself, not the reason why it's moving or what you think it's moving to. A more market neutral approach.

You can choose to trade with a narrative bias, you can choose to ignore bias, data, news everything external. It's your choice. I choose to accept what I know. What I can understand from everything out there and choose what I do with it.

Most of the time I will wait and trade the aftermath of any major data release. I am happy to use size and use a trade type that will get me less of the move while still being able to make money. It may not be the big money all the time or even ever again. One thing is for certain, I personally will never risk amounts that may lead to having another big loss on data.

14. HOW I MEASURE MY SUCCESS

I HAVE BEEN ABLE to do, within reason, whatever I wanted to do, whenever I wanted to do it, for a long time. That to me is success in life.

Now I'm not talking about going out and buying a Gulf Stream. This is why I have talked about goals and being realistic with your own expectations. I've been able to live my life the way I wanted to. I have the time I wanted, I have the things I wanted, I lead a very normal life with the people I choose to.

I feel I have the life I deserve for what I have put into it. I don't have too little, I don't feel like I have too much, I am exactly where I should be.

What do I put my success down to?

> "It ain't about how hard you hit. It's about how hard you can get hit and keep moving forward; how much

you can take and keep moving forward. That's how winning is done!"
–Rocky

People may scoff at that quote because of the film. Sylvester Stallone was an actor before *Rocky*. Not very famous. He wrote the script for himself to play the role, to become famous. Hollywood offered ever-increasing amounts to buy the script from him and to cast another actor. He held out until they finally agreed to let him be the star of the film. He backed himself. You have to give respect where it is due.

As cheesy as the words may be construed, they still hold meaning to me anyway. I don't have any problem with where I get my inspiration or how I find things that I connect with.

I don't have any problem with *success* or any of my *failures* in trading. No matter what happened along my journey I kept moving forward. I'm still moving forward. I don't feel I am, I know I am winning in life compared to a lot of people.

Maybe I'm not as pessimistic as I thought?

MEASURING MY TRADING SUCCESS

When measuring success in your trading it is down to you how you do it. I do it by, you guessed it, money. Going back to the recurring theme in this book, money is what all this was for.

As a pro retail trader I set a minimum monetary target for what I wanted to make each year from trading. This means money I want to use in the real world and spend. Not just numbers on a screen.

Once I have a base amount, I will then split that number into monthly, weekly and daily targets. These are only approximate targets. I set a minimum as there is an amount that makes it worthwhile in turning up to trade. If it's too high, too much pressure, too low, then what's the point? It's good to set big goals to see what you are potentially capable of. When you have done it for long enough you then know what you are actually capable of. The big goals motivated me to begin with, pushed me. I know what my current limits are. Do you?

I'm always amazed why traders do not even attempt to do anything as basic as this. If you don't have an overall goal, how are you going to get there? If you don't have targets to reach, how can you measure if you are getting there? It's just an endless road to nowhere.

I measure my trading success trade by trade, day by day, week by week, month by month, year by year. I don't over-complicate it. I don't change it until something needs changing. This can result from a big win or loss. I've traded for long enough to know that over a year, a certain number of trades and the ability to place a certain amount of size trades, means I will come out at a monetary level that I'm comfortable with.

It isn't more complicated than that. You can only measure trading success with money. You may want to use a percentage gain in the account, it's still money. It's the same thing.

Until the numbers make sense to you, until the process of setting goals and achieving those goals happens, trading can become meaningless. You don't seem to get anywhere.

The pro retail way of measuring life's success is taking money you have made and using it for real life, just like the pros. The pro retail way of measuring trading success is just like the pro traders. You make a minimum amount of money over a set amount of time.

15. MOMENTUM

MOMENTUM I HAVE left until last. This is a very underrated thing in trading. I treat it like I do when harnessing my emotions. It is something I must be consciously aware of. I know momentum is not an emotion, but I do class it as a feeling. It is a mental state, something pulling me forward.

Very much with finishing this book, which has been a long process and taken much more time than I had anticipated. I know, being the final chapter, this is important. I can visualise sending the final draft to the publisher. The anticipation of what people will make of it. All that momentum, the 40,000 or so words I've done so far, the momentum to finish is pulling me forward. Knowing what I have done in the past can be replicated, and this time I can do it bigger and better.

Like everything in this book regarding trading, I know it, because I have done it before.

It's one of the easiest things in trading to feel defeated. Especially for retail traders. One wrong split second decision can have both significant financial and emotional consequences. A massive loss of momentum.

Any loss of money in trading has an effect on all levels of traders, no matter how experienced or big they are. No trader likes to lose or to think they were wrong. It's how you deal with it.

What's even more frustrating in trading is that most traders are usually right, eventually, it's just the timing of the trade that was wrong. Every trader will lose at some point. It's simply part of trading. How you deal with losses can be more important than the loss itself.

This is the same with winning trades. There are ways to deal with winning in life or trading. You may have to get momentum back when you lose, you may have to control momentum when you win. I don't think there is such a thing as too much momentum, but too much of anything can be dangerous eventually.

Trading is all in your head. It's not a physical battle, it's a mental battle.

HOW I HARNESS MOMENTUM

I've been honest about the type of person I am. I'm quite pessimistic. I can't just replace that part of my personality with unbridled optimism. That's not who I am, I've accepted that. I have to replace my pessimistic nature in trading terms, results, money, with simple numbers. I know in a set time, if I do *x* number of trades over *y* amount of time I make *z* amounts of profits. More or less.

To some extent trading still has to be treated like a job. Some people go on about routines and mental health. Mantras, workouts, how to manifest your success. That's fine. You do you. My trading style, what money means to me, my personality, my purpose for doing what I do, is personal to me.

It's locked in a small compartment in my brain for only me to access. I don't, outside of what I'm writing now, allow many, if anyone, in there. That's for me. It's my creation and it's my responsibility. I don't attribute or try not to attribute my trading state based on how I'm feeling at any particular point in time.

We all have stuff going on in our lives. When it's time to trade, you should know if you are in the correct state or not, whatever that means in your own trading terms.

I know no matter what's going on in 'life' as a pro retail trader, my aim is to make money the best and fastest way I can from my trade types. Any other distraction should not factor when it's time to trade.

This is hard, as I've explained with the professional level environment you should create when pro retail trading. Nothing will ever be perfect. That's just what everyone has to come to terms with. You can only create the physical and mental space you are capable of.

I gain momentum by achieving my own goals. I want to do something, and I do it. It may not always be the way

I visualised it to be, and yes, I do visualise things, but I don't think that is anything new or groundbreaking. The one thing I do that most other people and traders do not is I own it. I live and die by my own sword. There are no congratulations needed when I do what I set out to do, there is no shoulder to cry on if it does not work.

While I have emotions and have explained how I harness them in trading, I don't have any emotional attachment to the end result of trading. Good or bad, I keep moving forward.

Trading and making money from trading is a lonely game. I am still a lone wolf when it comes to physically trading. Outside of trading life, along my journey I've had to compartmentalise this. I couldn't get to the level of trading and the size required on my own. I had to grow as a person to be able to grow as a trader.

Much of my early momentum was gained by things I wanted, then buying them. I've covered that in the motivation chapter. Motivation can be linked to momentum, but you have life momentum and trading momentum. You have to balance them out together to get the overall benefits.

Momentum is more powerful than motivation when you are doing well in trading. It is also one thing that I'm acutely aware of, and can come to a crashing halt.

GETTING MOMENTUM BACK

How many traders have been told: 'Go get a real job'?

This could be seen as a negative. It could be seen as a counterintuitive form of motivation. Reverse psychology? For me this is something *normal people* may say to a trader. Like everything I've explained in this book, unless you make your money or your income from trading is it really a profession, a job?

As I write this, I can feel the emotion it brings out in me. Get a job? How dare you! These are the things I tap into to get myself moving in the right direction. I've shown you, I'll show you again. Who am I showing? No one, just myself.

This phrase is personal to me. Early on in my trading career I did have to get a job. Well, it was offered to me. It's coupled with my fear and emotions in trading, which I harness. I don't want to ever go back to being *poor*, not that I was ever *poor*, but you know what I mean. I don't ever want to go back to working for anyone or being backed or simply not being in control of my own trading destiny.

I have to mentally engage the box in my brain, open the momentum drawer and do something I know in the past that has started the momentum ball rolling. Again, this is all part of the journey. I'm self-aware enough to know that at times even I need a boost. It can be something as simple as saying something to myself like: "Get a job Steve".

There are ways I deal with momentum:

1. What do I want? Let's aim to buy a thing. Even if I won't or don't buy it. It's a tool. It's just going back to my very first impulses, motivations and, more importantly, something I've done before. It's unlikely

to give me the same bump in momentum it has in the past. However, it's something, it's a start. Sometimes that's all I need.

2. Scalp. This is an instinct. I need to tap into one of my tried and tested states. Controlled rage. It doesn't have to be my biggest trade. It just has to be enough to make it mean something to me. It has, and still does, reawaken my somewhat primal trading needs. The resulting win or loss does engage my momentum. It's not about the money, it's about getting back in the game. Moving forward regardless of the cost.

3. Do something else. I trade at a level and a size where if the momentum is not working in my favour I'll just sit on my hands. I don't really have many hobbies.

   When I do something else, it will be trading related. I'll do something else that interests me but adds value to what I do as a trader. I would say writing this book. It's taken too long for that to be a short-term momentum boost. Starting a book would count. It's many more things like speaking to other traders. People I know, who do what I do. Recharge the ego. There is nothing like a bit of friendly trader rivalry to get things moving in your head.

4. Boredom. This is not to be confused with a boredom trade. I have, and you can, physically get to a place where life is so tragically tedious that no matter how bad you think your trading has been, there is only one

> way out. To trade. It's almost like I create the desire again. I can force myself to take a break from trading, not for too long, but long enough for me to feel I have the right and need to trade again.

It doesn't matter on the size at the start, you just have to do it. It just has to be the only logical option to get back to doing, to creating momentum.

This may seem a bit extreme and a bit out there. These things are what make the pro part in anything that's hard to do. Simply keep doing what you've done in the past, which over time has worked. You will be rewarded for it. Keep going. No matter how you choose to do it, keep moving forward.

WHEN YOU'RE UP IN TRADING AND LIFE

This is where the pro and pro retail traders and retail traders can get things very wrong.

Momentum when you are winning in trading or life can be dangerous. Nothing lasts forever and it's easy when things come quickly, like trading profits, for people to fully accept that. Money in life can go very quickly if you get it too easily.

I'll break it down to the pro world and the retail world.

PRO WORLD MOMENTUM

In the pro world success in trading can spill out very quickly into real life. It is infectious and can be consuming. This is one of the reasons the floor lost its appeal to me. It's a very ego-driven male environment and men with money, at their most basic level, are mostly the same. Traders on the floor are deep down all the same. We like a good time.

There is a huge positive to this and the floor environment. When the dust settles and you've partied like a pro, the momentum you then expect from yourself and from the others who have no doubt heard about it, maybe even been there with you, means you have two options. You play with profit and scale up and aim to make the same or more, or you do the exact opposite and do nothing. You sit on your hands, and you wait for the next opportunity.

This level of momentum is only really ever seen at a pro level. All pro traders, again I know I'm repeating myself, have a big win or big winning streak story. I suppose it doesn't have to be a big win to gain momentum, but as I've explained, what else is there but money in the pro world? I can't name a non-related trading one. There are key amounts of money and time frames that warrant attention. Amounts that would be worthy of crediting any momentum to. This is in the tens of thousands in minutes, hours or days range.

The best traders will use this profit to make more profit. Use more size. Wait for the same or better opportunity. This takes an enormous amount of experience and discipline. While I've experienced traders go out and do wild things, it's the best traders that know the momentum you get from trading with profits. It is one of the few chances you can have to play with anything close to resembling what non-traders may think of as *free money*.

In all, momentum for pro traders is a different thing when they are doing well from that of retail traders. Most pro traders will put money away for inevitable bad times. They know that as quick as the money comes in, it can go. If you have traded for long enough, you have been through the stages of a trading journey, which includes all the things I personally have done and bought etc.

The best pro traders use money as a backstop where momentum becomes less important because it's factored into the overall goals. It's part of the profession, career, their long-term plan.

RETAIL WORLD MOMENTUM

In the retail world you are much more insular. This is why you see retail traders on social media and in chat rooms. They need to show they are worthy of the success they have had. They are not surrounded by their supposed peers on the floor.

This can be said for the pro retail trader also. You are in a precarious position where you can make seemingly incredible amounts of money, but who is there to share that experience with you? From my own experience, no one. Well, no one who gets it.

So where does the momentum come from and what do you do to get it back?

Retail traders will invariably try to replicate that same trade and do it quickly. This is a common mistake. Most of their momentum comes from making money that comes from larger pip wins, on smaller size and over longer periods of time. These trades are hard enough to spot in the first place. Even if you do get the right entry and hold it for enough time, yes they are great wins to have. Are they wins you can replicate again? Immediately again? No.

Most retail traders will let emotions or inexperience of big wins or losses spill over into their momentum or overall journey. It turns into over-confidence. I don't see momentum ever working for retail traders in the same way it will for a pro or pro retail trader. As I've tried to explain, most never get anywhere near the *pro* level and all that entails.

There is very rarely the plan element or overall goals and targets to keep the over-confidence in check, thinking they have cracked trading and it's going to carry on. The best thing to do after any big win, good run, any momentum you have gained, is to stop trading. It does not have to be for long, but as quick as retail traders get momentum it goes.

When momentum goes for retail traders they will try to regain it with size or by adding time to trades. This very rarely ends well.

Retail traders can't physically trade like pro traders. It doesn't mean they can't trade to a pro level in a retail environment to an extent. The *pro* part of pro retail trading comes from a combination of everything I've experienced and written in this book.

16. GOING FORWARD

To be successful in trading, how you place your trades and make money must be personal to you.

In my experience, people and most traders want to be told what to do, shown how it's done. There is no single guaranteed way to do this. The only thing guaranteed is that if you do not know yourself, trust yourself, prove to yourself you can do it, you will ultimately never make money trading.

Everyone's trading journey is different but essentially has the same steps along the way. It comes down to how you deal with the inevitable losses and manage your expectations when you win. You will always learn more about yourself losing trades than winning them.

I've had to look back at things like my motivations and revisit them. This is why the motivation section came later in the book.

During the course of writing this book, thinking back to how I felt when I experienced things, I have to remember that not everyone knows what I know. If you haven't traded before, you will have to do this as you go. Make mental notes for the future.

Less is more in trading. Talk to other traders. Talk to other people who have 'it'. Don't get bogged down in groups and forums. Trading can be isolating, but you need to embrace that rather than look for some collective validation.

Have goals. Make them achievable. Reward yourself when you achieve them. Make the money real.

Trading is the easiest thing in the world to do. It is simply the click of a button. The less you battle with your emotions, your ego or self-doubt, the quicker you will do what every trader sets out to do, not matter what they tell you, which is to make money.

Be a free thinker. Make your own decisions on what you believe is best for you. No one can truly know how they will react or feel until they do it.

There are rules in everything, for a reason. Some for the right reason, some for other reasons. Only you can be the trader you want to be. No one can do that for you. It's only people who play by their own rules who get to play a different part of the game.

I don't pretend to have all the answers. I have pushed the limits of what I thought I could achieve in trading. Sometimes it has worked and sometimes it has not. When you push yourself to the extreme, you can always pull back.

If you never push the boundaries, you will always just stay where you are.

No matter what you experience in trading, you have to keep going. Never give in.

Trading is a game where there are no take-backs. You are only as good as your last trade. What trade do you want that to be?

The end.